Franco-Ontarians feel that they are both part of and rejected by Canada's two founding peoples. Although proud of their heritage, many hide the French side of their lives from the surrounding English majority. Some are pessimistic about their future; but for many in the region commonly known as Nouvel-Ontario, French roots run deep.

For more than a year and a half Sheila Arnopoulos travelled through the region visiting or living in Sudbury, Hearst, Dubreuilville, and Timmins. Here she chronicles the changes time has brought to the lives of some of the 700,000 people of French origin in Ontario. She describes the blossoming of a culture which draws from both French and English backgrounds. She features the stories of two celebrated Canadian businessmen from Sudbury, Paul Desmarais and Robert Campeau, in a discussion of the development of a new commercial and financial élite. Arnopoulos also writes of miners, poets, playwrights, lumber barons, and ordinary people, to give a vivid picture of their frustrations and aspirations.

The French of Nouvel-Ontario have created a regional identity of their own. But under what conditions can French communities in English Canada hope to survive? Arnopoulos finds that federal bilingualism and the expansion of French Quebec businesses across the country are most likely the key factors.

Sheila McLeod Arnopoulos is co-author with Dominique Clift of *The English Fact in Quebec*, winner of the 1979 Governor-General's Award for non-fiction in its French edition. A journalist at the *Montreal Star* for ten years, she received a National Newspaper Award for her series on immigrants. Long concerned with English / French relations, she is the only anglophone member of the Quebec government's Conseil de la langue française.

Sheila McLeod Arnopoulos

Voices from French Ontario

McGill-Queen's University Press
Kingston and Montreal

© McGill-Queen's University Press 1982
ISBN 0-7735-0405-2 (cloth)
ISBN 0-7735-0406-0 (paper)

Legal deposit 4th quarter 1982
Bibliothèque nationale du Québec

Printed in Canada

A French translation of this work has been published under the title
Hors du Québec point de salut? by Éditions Libre Expression,
244 St. James Street West, Montreal, Quebec H2Y 1L9.

Cover photographs by Jules Villemaire, Ottawa.
Workers in the lumber industry, Hearst, Ontario (left, above and below),
and members of Théâtre Les Franco-folles, Sudbury, Ontario.

Canadian Cataloguing in Publication Data

Arnopoulos, Sheila McLeod.
  Voices from French Ontario

  Includes index.
  Bibliography: p.
  ISBN 0-7735-0405-2 (bound). – ISBN 0-7735-0406-0 (pbk.)

  1. Canadians, French-speaking – Ontario.* 2. Canadians,
  French-speaking – Ontario – Sudbury.* 3. Canada –
  English–French relations. I. Title.
  FC3100.5.A75   971.3'1004114   C82-095048-3
  F1059.7.F8A75

54,415

The excerpt from E.J. Pratt's poem "Towards the Last Spike" is reprinted
by kind permission of University of Toronto Press.

This book has been published with the assistance of the Canada
Council under its block grant program.

The Canada Council
Conseil des Arts du Canada
1957-1982

Contents

that is helping Nouvel-Ontario participate more fully in urban and industrial activities.

Even though education in French is now available to the end of high school, the school question continues to worry many Franco-Ontarians. They want separate French schools administered by autonomous French school boards. The provincial government refuses to make these a matter of fundamental rights.

Federal bilingualism has confirmed the legitimacy of French and consolidated the cultural identity of Franco-Ontarians. But their feelings of insecurity persist because the concessions they have obtained from the Ontario government have not been accompanied by recognition of French as an official language in the province.

Many young Franco-Ontarians are attracted to English because the ideas and activities associated with it seem more interesting. French culture does not offer the same variety. Personal ambition and the lure of a more enriching life gradually wear away the cultural and linguistic loyalties of young Franco-Ontarians.

Ignored by the elite of their own community, the French miners in Sudbury sought refuge in a left-wing union that was labelled communist. The miners played a historic role in keeping one of the most progressive unions in North America from becoming totally absorbed into the Steelworkers union.

Lumbering operations in northern Ontario are dominated by a dozen francophone entrepreneurs who, from humble beginnings, built up impressive businesses. All came originally from Quebec but now consider themselves to be full-fledged members of the Franco-Ontarian community.

Chapter 9
Tycoons from Sudbury 147
The phenomenal success of Paul Desmarais and Robert Campeau, two businessmen from Sudbury, can be explained in large part by the flexibility they acquired in dealing on a daily basis with the French and the English, and by the fact that they were not weighed down by strong traditions.

Epilogue
The French Connection 165
The new commercial and financial elite of Nouvel-Ontario will undoubtedly become part of the growing French economic network of Quebec that is expanding across Canada and the United States. In addition, its members will become indispensable links between head offices in Toronto and Montreal.

Appendix
The Marginal Man 169
Some theoretical background from the literature of sociology helps explain the nature and role of the hybrid, or bicultural, personality prevalent in Franco-Ontario.

Supplementary Maps

Tables

Preface

When I first arrived in Sudbury to do research for this book on Franco-Ontarians in the north, people I met wanted to know why an anglophone from Quebec would be interested in them. Francophones from Quebec had come with microphones and television cameras, especially after the Parti Québécois came to power in 1976. But as people from Sudbury explained, it was only to find out how diminished they were by assimilation, and to predict when they might roll over and die. Quebecers, they said, wanted to promote the cause of independence by demonstrating that French culture outside the province was doomed. "Don't talk to me about assimilation," said Monique Cousineau, the director of the Centre des jeunes, when I showed up at her office the first day. "We're fed up talking with people from Quebec about that." I quickly discovered that a Quebec writer in Sudbury was always cause for apprehension. As an English Quebecer, I was in a category apart, but since my intentions were not known, I was also suspect.

There is a long preamble to my interest in the French minority in northern Ontario. Some of it is professional and academic, but much of it is personal. During the 1970s, when I was a journalist at the *Montreal Star*, I could not avoid becoming caught up in the growing conflict between the French and English in Montreal. Shortly after the Parti Québécois came to power—when many leaders in the anglophone community believed the English would never be accepted in the new Quebec—I wrote a series of articles on anglophones who were integrating into Quebec society by choosing to work in French. I was fascinated to see how certain members of the English minority were reconciling themselves to the French majority rather than resisting it. I was curious to find out more about people who were trying to move toward a bicultural consciousness.

While some people found the articles interesting, the series was not well received by the various elites of the anglophone community who seemed to believe that French and English were mutually exclusive states of being. However, I was, and still am, convinced that a harmonization of English and French cultures is the only option for anglophones who intend to stay in Quebec.

I went on to write a master's thesis in sociology on the English community in Montreal. From there I collaborated on a book with fellow writer Dominique Clift on relations between the English minority and the French majority in Quebec. Called *The English Fact in Quebec*, it did not find an English publisher until after the appearance of the French translation, which in 1980 won the Governor General's literary award. But the book did not please the anglophone community in Montreal because it challenged the wisdom of the English elite's efforts to maintain its old role in Quebec.

We pointed out that the rise of nationalism in Quebec has not been easy for anglophones to accept. The French majority in Quebec are in charge, and the English must adjust to its restrictive language policies. In most professions they must pass French tests before they can practise, for example, and, with minor exceptions, cannot use English signs in their businesses. Across Canada the press has strongly criticized the Quebec government for its treatment of the English. Yet there is another minority in the country about which very little has been written: the French outside Quebec.

The French communities across Canada have little in common with the English minority in Quebec. They have another history and cultural problems of a completely different order. But they make up an essential element of Canada. Their collective experience reflects a prevalent Canadian condition: the confused and often antagonistic way that the two founding peoples relate to one another.

In Canada we have always thought that French and English were very different, and in many ways they are. Yet the more closely I examine the nature of the two cultures, the more I believe that we are inextricably bound at the psychological level. Deeply concerned about survival, Canadians of French and English origin project their feelings of insecurity upon one another. Torn by ambiguous attitudes, their hate for each other can be as fierce as their attachment.

Those who long most for a stabilization of relations between the two groups, for some sort of compromise, are French Ontarians and a growing group of English Quebecers. These people do not think that their *pays*, or country, is somewhere else. A francophone from Sudbury does not consider Quebec his homeland any more than I see Ontario as mine. Living successfully as a member of a minority often means living in two cultures. Unfortunately, the pure-bred English and French of the two provinces tend to consider bicultural people as mutants that should not be encouraged to flourish. Consequently, many of these people find themselves living in a disturbing no-man's land—a world that I was eager to explore.

It is my continuing preoccupation with this dual personality—the divided self, if you will—that attracted me to the French communities of northern Ontario. I was keen to understand how francophones in Ontario balance minority living with participation in the English world around them. I also wanted to gain a greater understanding of the francophone world which fuels the other side of my own cultural consciousness. And perhaps I wanted a glimpse at my own future.

This, then, is why I spent eighteen months going back and forth between Sudbury and Montreal. I selected Ontario as a place of research because it contains the largest number of francophones outside Quebec. However, I felt I would gain an intimate understanding of Franco-Ontarians only if I focused upon a particular region. I therefore chose to concentrate upon the area called Nouvel-Ontario in the northern part of the province. Francophones make up about one-quarter of the total population of the north. Originally from Quebec, they began to arrive in the late nineteenth century when the Canadian Pacific Railway opened up the area to colonization. The first migrants settled on the land; those who came later worked in lumber camps and mines. Sudbury, which is one-third French, has always been their cultural capital. Links with north-western Quebec remain strong, but the people of Nouvel-Ontario feel they have a distinct culture which sets them apart from Quebec.

During my frequent visits to Sudbury I boarded with the Franco-Ontarian family of Henri and Thérèse Brunet, who provided me with many insights into their community. I also spent several weeks travelling by bus across the north, interviewing people in predominantly French towns such as Hearst, Timmins, and Dubreuilville. Between trips I spent weeks reading Franco-Ontarian literature.

My experiences in Nouvel-Ontario revealed to me the world of the north, with its proximity to nature and its tough frontier living. Coming from the bustling city of Montreal, I was like a stranger in a new country and it took me a long time before I felt I was getting close to Franco-Ontarian culture. Although many people were friendly and welcomed me, others were very reserved. "We don't like being studied," explained a teacher, who was defensive about investigations into Franco-Ontarian life. "It's as if there's something not right about us."

My account of the people of Nouvel-Ontario has been written with the eye of an anglophone from Quebec, and this, without doubt, has influenced how I have told their story. As an outsider there are probably many things that I have overlooked or misunderstood, but I have done my best to capture the feelings and spirit of the region. I have not attempted to write the complete story of Nouvel-Ontario in all its historical detail; rather, I have tried to describe certain aspects of a community that is undergoing and adapting to growth and change. I hope that in so doing I have been able to relive for the reader some of the excitement and difficulties that francophones are experiencing in communities outside Quebec. There is an adage that says that nations are judged by the way they treat their minorities. How the francophones in a region like Nouvel-Ontario are preserving their culture reveals a great deal about the nature of Canada.

Acknowledgements

The author thanks Dominique Clift, Josh Freed, Susan Blaylock, and Mark Wilson for their comments and suggestions. Special recognition is due John Gilmore for helping prepare the manuscript for publication.

Research for this book was made possible by a grant from the Canadian Human Rights Foundation. The views expressed in the book are those of the author, and not necessarily those of the foundation.

Map of Nouvel-Ontario

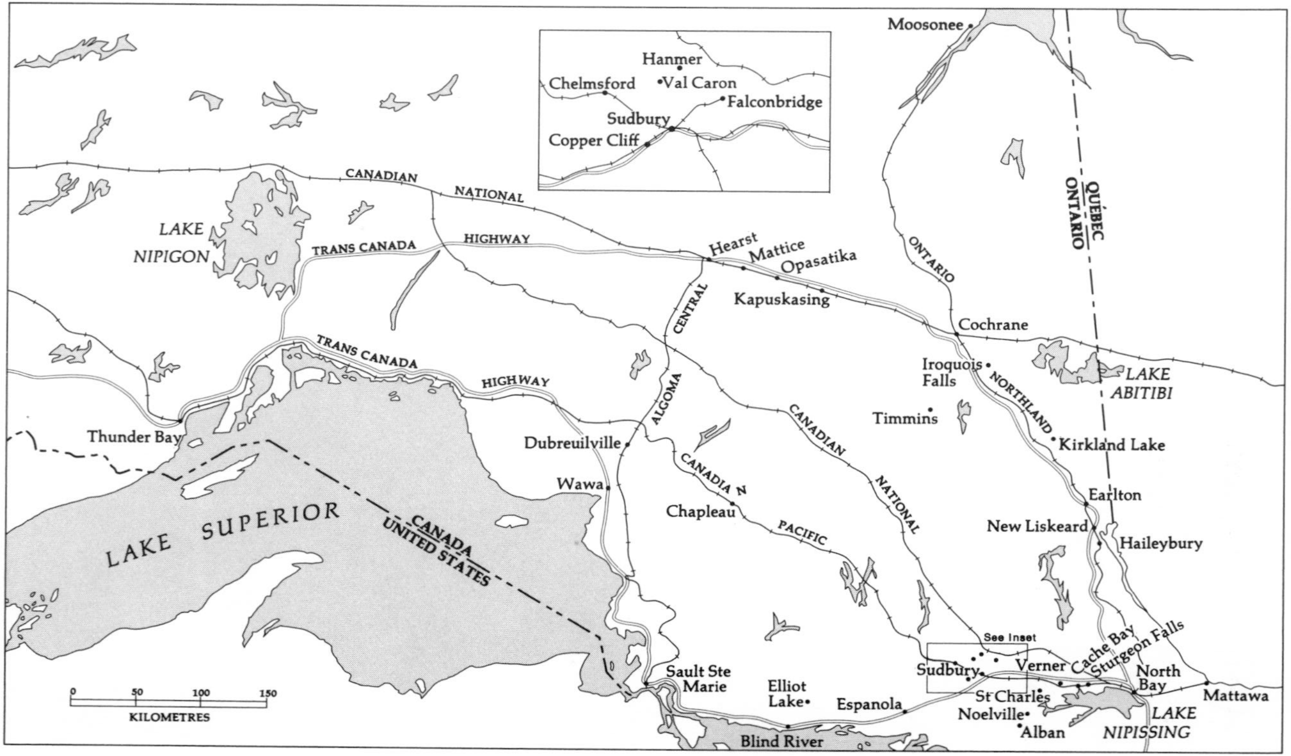

Voices from
French Ontario

Chapter 1

Au nord de notre vie

Our country is the North
          WHERE
solitude erodes the tender heart
ore of the earth
of rock, forest and cold
          WE
are stubborn and subterranean
in solidarity our stony cries
rise to the four winds
of the possible future

Robert Dickson, poster poem, 1975[1]

The Contradictions of Nouvel-Ontario

It was a cool spring night in Sudbury as students carrying knapsacks poured in from across Ontario for one of the major Franco-Ontarian festivals of the year: *La nuit sur l'étang*, the night on the frog pond. Across Canada the word *frog* is often used as a derogatory term for French Canadians, but in Sudbury during *La nuit sur l'étang* it has become a symbol for a new French pride. In the words of Marie-Paule, a curly-haired student fresh off the bus from Hearst: "This is the night when we sit on our lily pads and sing to one another all night long. It's when we stop fighting being frogs—when we celebrate being French. I come to *La nuit sur l'étang* every year. I'd never miss it."

Marie-Paule was one of hundreds of students who had come to Laurentian University in Sudbury to join the rock stars, poets, and playwrights of Franco-Ontario in a two-day celebration of being French. An annual event which started in 1973 in the heyday of the community's own Quiet Revolution, *La nuit sur l'étang* attracts French-speaking youth from as far away as the Maritimes and Manitoba. Most of the participants, however, come from Nouvel-Ontario—the homeland of the Franco-Ontarians whose roots lie in the farms, logging camps, and mines in the north of the province. This is an area roughly bounded by Sudbury, North Bay, Hearst, Thunder Bay, and Sault Ste. Marie. The name Nouvel-Ontario was coined at the turn of the century by both French and

English to differentiate the northern frontier territory of Ontario from the more developed south. Eventually the English dropped the name, but the French continue to use it with pride to refer to their growing frontier community.

In 1980 the highlight of *La nuit sur l'étang* was a concert by Robert Paquette, Sudbury's home-grown folk-rock star who can whip up a crowd as no outsider can. Paquette now lives in Montreal, but in the early 1970s he was part of a commune of writers and musicians in Sudbury that produced a series of controversial French rock operas which paved the way for a permanent French theatre in Sudbury.

Wearing a wide-brimmed straw hat, Paquette strummed a few notes on his guitar and launched into a song from his album *Prends celui qui passe* as the crowd rose in a great wave and cheered wildly. Paquette sings in French, but like many *chansonniers* from outside Quebec, his music is a curious mixture of Scottish balladry, American blues and rock, and the French *chansonnier* tradition. Sometimes sentimental, often harsh, they reflect the will of francophones outside Quebec to thrive. Paquette is so popular in Nouvel-Ontario that the youth know many of his songs by heart. At one point in the concert he stopped singing, but the band kept on playing and the audience swayed to the music and sang verse after verse, without missing a word.

Until five in the morning, Paquette and a host of other rock singers, poets, jazz musicians, and blue-grass bands kept the audience enraptured. Between performances, crowds spilled out into the lobby of the theatre to examine art exhibits and kiosques of books by Franco-Ontarians. One book which attracted special attention was *La parole et la loi*, a play about the history and social consequences of Regulation 17, which closed French schools in Ontario from 1912 to 1927. A couple of students who had seen the play were leafing through the book. "*Tiens, écoute, c'est là que nous en sommes!* This sums up where we're at," said a girl from Sturgeon Falls. As she read aloud, a crowd gathered.

It's up to each one of us
to make our history.
Let's face it, we're sick
of being just a minority

of getting bogged down in the past,
we have to learn to look ahead.

We've had to search for our identity
so long that we can hardly breathe.
Don't talk to us about assimilation any more,
or about a people on the verge of extinction.

We thought we'd tell you of the struggles of the past,
for those who don't know of it, or have forgotten.
But believe us, in the next show
there won't be any talk about history and the past—
and we hope you'll be there to share it with us.[2]

This closing song from the play contains a powerful and important message for Franco-Ontarians—one that is reinforced by almost every performance at La nuit sur l'étang—vivre plutôt que survivre, let's live rather than just survive.

Only a few kilometres away from Laurentian University is working-class Moulin à Fleur, the most French part of Sudbury. This is a community of miners. Jagged hills of black rock without a tree or a patch of grass bear down upon the neighbourhood. Far in the distance, from the massive Inco smelter, rises the towering smoke stack that has made Sudbury famous. During the 1950s, Moulin à Fleur—named after the old flour mill that still stands on the main street—was a slum with draughty houses and cracked sidewalks. Since then, the miners' salaries have risen and the community has made improvements. Moulin à Fleur is now a modest but attractive neighbourhood of manicured cottages.

Moulin à Fleur is predominantly French. But unlike the youth who celebrate their culture at La nuit sur l'étang, residents of this community hide their language and identity. Two buildings in the community are unmistakably French: one, Saint-Jean-de-Brébeuf church with its tall spire, handsome brick presbytery, and gleaming stained glass windows; the other, the caisse populaire. Manager Arthur Pharand remembers clearly when the caisse first opened in 1949. The Ontario government sent a civil servant up from Toronto who demanded that the minutes of the credit union be written in English as well as French, but the *caisse populaire* members—all of whom were French—were appalled. They put up such a fuss about the use of English that the civil servant finally withdrew his request. Today, the *caisse*'s minutes are still kept in French only.

The church and the *caisse* aside, Moulin à Fleur presents an English face to the world. A handful of establishments like Nolin's garage, Bradley's pharmacy, and the Banque Nationale have bilingual signs, but the remainder have little or no French character. Typical is Legacé's Confectionary Ltd. and Pastry Shop, one of the oldest and most popular shops in Moulin à Fleur. Though most of the clientele is French, there is not one French sign to be seen. Outside, donuts, sandwiches, and submarines are advertised in English. Inside, the only hint that the store might be French is a stack of French birthday cards and an imposing assortment of pastel and gold statues of the Virgin Mary and St. Joseph, peering down from high shelves.

When I dropped in for a visit one Saturday morning, there were about ten people in the store and the radio was tuned to an English station. A young French miner picked a lighter off the rack and plunked it on the counter by the cash. "*C'est tout?*" asked the cashier. "That'll be one fifty-nine, please," she said in English. Other people arrived at the counter with drinks and sandwiches. "Is that all?" she asked, again in English. After the customers left, the cashier called out to the owner, Guy Legacé, at the front of the shop, and in English asked him about some merchandise. Bewildered, I asked Legacé—in French—why he was talking English to his French-speaking cashier. "Well," he said, speaking French in a near-whisper, "it's a very delicate matter. If there are English people around—even if the conversation doesn't concern them—we speak English. It's more comfortable that way. Why don't we put up French signs outside? Well ... the English wouldn't like it. Moulin à Fleur may be French, but English people drop in here." He shrugged his shoulders with an air of resignation. "This *is* Ontario," he said.

Legacé talked in a matter-of-fact way about the situation, but he obviously found the question painful. Born in Quebec, he has lived most of his life in Moulin à Fleur. Long ago he became accustomed to repressing his French nature in public. Like many other small businessmen, he is active in French community

6

groups like the Club Richelieu, where he is president. Treating me like a fellow francophone who understands the dilemma of the French in Sudbury, he continued talking in French. "In Sudbury, we have to go to completely French places to feel at ease speaking French. That's why we have the Club Richelieu, the Centre des jeunes, and the Club Alouette."

Next door to Legacé's Confectionary is Tammy's Savings Centre, a popular second-hand store. Among the signs hanging outside were: Clothing for the Entire Family; I Believe in Recycling; and Furniture, Appliances, Clothing, Baby Furniture. "We didn't have room for French signs," said Hélène Ross, a seventeen-year-old French girl from the predominantly French town of Val Caron, ten miles from Sudbury. "*Les Canadiens-Français comprennent l'anglais mais les Anglais comprennent pas le français.* The French understand English, but the English don't understand French," she explained. Hélène's mother and aunt, both of them French, started the store in 1972. "There are people on welfare in Moulin à Fleur who can use a store like this; that's why we opened it."

The phone rang and Hélène answered: "Hello? Tammy's." "You never know," she said afterward, "sometimes it's someone English. We sell on consignment and English people bring things in. When we speak French, the English get mad. Once I was speaking to a customer in French and by mistake I continued in French to another woman who turned out to be English." At this point Hélène drew herself up into a caricature of the infuriated English matron. Her voice reflected the comedy of the situation, but her eyes showed her horror at the memory of the confrontation. "The woman snapped: 'Look, if you want to run a French store, go to Quebec,' and walked out." Hélène took a deep breath and then paused. "We certainly want to avoid situations like that," she said with emphasis. At seventeen, Hélène already knows what is expected of French people in Sudbury and accepts the situation despite its obvious discomforts. "Oh well," she said, trying to dismiss the matter. "I've seen the other side of the coin in Rouyn, Québec, where I have relatives. There the French don't want to hear any English."

The joyous celebration of French culture at *La nuit sur l'étang* and the symptoms of withdrawal manifested in Moulin à Fleur reflect two aspects of French consciousness in Nouvel-Ontario. Sudbury writer André Paiement was painfully aware of this duality. His ballet adaptation of Molière's *Le malade imaginaire* expresses the contradiction of Franco-Ontarian life this way: "*Schizophrénie! Schizophrénie!* You will *bien vouloir excuser* our *manière de parler, mais nous comprenons* what we say. *Schizophrénie! Schizophrénie!* Is what we be."

Minorities such as the Franco-Ontarians who participate in two cultures and speak two languages often suffer inner conflict. There is the exhilaration of searching for a cultural identity in opposition to the majority and the satisfaction of moving freely from one culture to the other. But there is also a feeling of power-lessness when they are denied the official recognition they feel they deserve.

In Canada there are about one million francophones—people whose mother tongue is French—living outside Quebec. More than half of them live in Ontario. Two-thirds of Ontario's French population live in the north-east around Sudbury and in the east around Ottawa; the other third lives in southern pockets around Toronto. Although French schools exist in southern Ontario, the French population there is too dispersed to establish many community services and is rapidly being assimilated into English culture.

The Ottawa area has managed to maintain a certain French spirit. Francophones in the eastern counties of Prescott, Russell, and Glengarry see Ottawa as a regional capital because the city offers employment in the civil service, the daily newspaper *Le Droit*, and the bilingual University of Ottawa, as well as a French cultural life which benefits from the city's proximity to Quebec. But the people of the region feel strongly ambivalent about Quebec: they want it to be dynamic and prosperous, but they do not consider themselves exiles who will one day return to their place of origin. On the contrary, they consider themselves Franco-Ontarians, with their own distinct history and identity.

Ottawa poet Jean-Marc Dalpé captures this feeling of belong-ing to Franco-Ontario in the final stanzas of his book, *Les murs de nos villages.*

Les Murs de nos villages recall
Les Murs de nos villages remember

our roots
that bite as deep in this land
as those of the oak

. . . .

Les violons de nos villages
sigh and scream
and belt out jigs like calls for freedom
and each note
torn from their strings
says
Here, we are at home.[3]

Sudbury has a shorter and less illustrious history than Ottawa, but for many francophones the city has a more appealing character. Now one-third French, it has become the regional capital of Nouvel-Ontario. The city was founded in 1883 when the Canadian Pacific Railway arrived to lay track for the transcontinental railway. Labourers from Quebec came in search of work, followed closely by the Jesuit priests who supplied the French population with a religious and social framework. The French named the site Sainte-Anne-des-Pins because of the surrounding pine forest; later a British railway superintendent renamed it Sudbury after his wife's village in England.

The opening of the railway encouraged the exploitation of northern Ontario's minerals and forests, and assured the rapid development of Sudbury and other towns such as Timmins, Kapuskasing, Kirkland Lake, and Hearst. Around the turn of the century the French settled on farms north of North Bay along the Ontario Northland Railway; many also worked in the lumber camps and mines. None of the French ever rose to positions of importance in the mining companies. Instead they distinguished themselves in the mining union movement, particularly during the bitter fight between Mine-Mill and the United Steelworkers of America in the 1950s and 1960s. Their militancy assured the precarious survival of Mine-Mill, which the rich and bureaucratic rival union tried to crush. Since then, French miners have become so influential in Mine-Mill that they determine who becomes president. Francophones also made their mark in the lumber industry, first in Sudbury, and later in Hearst, Timmins, and Dubreuilville. Today, the sawmill industry in Ontario is dominated by a dozen, prosperous French-speaking lumber barons.

In 1913 cultural and intellectual life in Nouvel-Ontario took a new turn when the Jesuits established the Collège du Sacré-Coeur in Sudbury to rival the University of Ottawa, founded by the Oblate Order of France. Hector Bertrand, editor of Sudbury's weekly Le Voyageur and a Jesuit himself, was an early student at the college. "I was brought up in Warren, and I must admit that when I entered Sacré-Coeur, my French was poor. When I came out, I could—and can—compete with any educated French-speaking person anywhere."

Over the years, a Nouvel-Ontario spirit was forged out of the frontier experience of French people on the farms and in the mines and lumber camps. An important dimension of Nouvel-Ontario history has been their will to survive as a distinct community. For Franco-Ontarians, language, religion, and ethnic origin are inextricably linked, and they have fought to preserve their identity against overwhelming odds. In 1912, the Ontario government passed Regulation 17 prohibiting French public education. At the same time, Irish Catholics did everything in their power to curb the development of French Catholic private schools, hospitals, and even parishes that functioned in French. Throughout their history, the French in Ontario had to battle on two fronts simultaneously: against the Protestant Orangemen, who were anti-Catholic, and the Irish Catholics, who were anti-French.

Since the late 1960s the status of the Franco-Ontarians has improved, largely because of the rise of French power in Ottawa and the fear of Quebec independence. Until 1969 there were no French public high schools in Ontario. In 1982 there were four in the Sudbury area alone. There have been improvements in other fields as well. With the enactment of the federal government's Official Languages Act in 1969, first federal and then provincial services began to be offered in French. In 1972 Sudbury was declared a bilingual city by the municipal government. The federal Secretary of State and the Ontario Arts Council began pouring thousands of dollars into French cultural activities. In 1978, Radio-Canada opened a French radio station in Sudbury.

These developments have changed the lives of people in Nouvel-Ontario. "A decade ago, French-speaking people did not have much of a French life in Sudbury," noted Anita Brunet-Lamarche of Sudbury's Prise de Parole publishing house. "Years ago, my father had to change his name from Lucien Brunet to Lou Brunet. He had to conceal his French identity to get a job. But that era is over." Nevertheless, the French community is haunted by memories of Regulation 17. The generation that endured the infamous legislation is afraid it will one day wake up to find French schools and other services wiped away by the English-speaking majority with the stroke of a legislative pen. "We have no real constitutional guarantees," complained Henri Brunet, a retired schoolteacher and former president of the Association canadienne-française de l'Ontario (AFCO) in Sudbury.[4]

Many Franco-Ontarians do not believe that the changes they have seen are permanent. Their feelings are reinforced by the large number of anglophones in Sudbury who think the French should behave as an ethnic group rather than as one of Canada's two founding peoples. This point of view is expressed frequently by the *Sudbury Star*, the only English daily in the city, which has opposed moves to make French an official language in Ontario. It is reflected in other domains as well. For example: in spite of the fact that Sudbury is officially bilingual, it is only rarely that any of its mayors have given speeches in French. In the same vein, French federal services are often only token. Air Canada has been known to tell French callers to call back four hours later "when a bilingual clerk is available." It is because of behaviour such as this that the people of Moulin à Fleur do not insist on using their language in public and often hide it away like an embarrassing relative.

The behaviour of minorities — whether as individuals or groups — is filled with contradictions. Minorities can be bold one moment and submissive the next. They can soar like birds, but they can also cower like children when scolded for stepping out of place. Minorities long to be separate and distinct from the majority that envelops them, but curiously, they often want to be part of that majority too. Sudbury playwright and actor Robert Marinier found out just how attached he was to both English and French communities when he arrived in Montreal in 1973 to study at the National Theatre School of Canada and found himself in a completely French environment. He missed not being able to live some of his life in English. "Montreal was a terrible cultural shock," he said. "One of the things that blew my mind was meeting French people who couldn't speak English."

Many of the French in Ontario show strong affinities to both languages and cultures. Almost 100,000 people in Ontario declared for the 1971 census that both French and English were their mother tongues. Many discover they have both a French self and an English self, which surface according to the environment and the occasion. Some find their English and French personalities are at war, while others keep them at peace. "I'm not a bicultural person," noted Gérard Lafrenière, head of Laurentian University's French program on the co-operative movement. "That would mean I was suffering from a divided self. No, I'm a hybrid. I may be a curious sort of Canadian beast, but it suits me."

Regrettably, the English / French hybrid has never been accepted in Canada. This poses psychological problems for francophones outside Quebec and, more recently, for certain anglophones in Quebec. Novels and poetry often reveal as much about cultural currents as do political speeches or letters to the editors. Ronald Sutherland, who teaches at the University of Sherbrooke, in Quebec, points out in his book *Second Image*, a comparative study of French and English literature in Canada, that both cultures have shown a marked degree of ethnocentrism, or what he refers to as "the body-odour of race," in their respective literatures.

This, he says, is different from the approach shown by American writers such as Mark Twain in *Huckleberry Finn* and Herman Melville in *Moby Dick*, who focused upon communion between persons of different races. "These writers, it would seem, either concluded or sensed that the realization of the American dream, indeed the survival of the American nation, would depend upon the ability of people of different ethnic origins to learn to live with each other in a mutually satisfactory manner."[5]

Sutherland observes that the English and French in Canada see their cultures as fundamentally opposed and do not approve of mixing the two. He takes Lionel Groulx's novel, *L'Appel de la race*, written in 1922, as typical of a cultural stance he believes is still to be found among both French and English in Canada. *L'Appel de la race* is about Jules de Lantagnac, a French-speaking member of Parliament who marries an English Canadian and experiences the dissolution of his home over his decision to oppose publicly Regulation 17. Lantagnac's four children eventually split into cultural camps, siding with either their father or their mother. At a crucial point in the book Lantagnac discerns in his children "a kind of unhealthy imprecision, a disorder of thought, and incoherence of the intellect ... It was as if they had in them two souls, two warring spirits which alternately dominated."[6] Groulx states in the book that "the effect of interbreeding between different races is to destroy the racial soul," and uses the theories of Joseph Arthur de Gobineau and other racial ideologues of the day to condemn marriages between English and French.[7] English-Canadian writers such as Susanna Moodie, in *Roughing It in the Bush*, reflect this same kind of obsessive concern for the maintenance of cultural purity.

Today, French and English fiction writers no longer reflect this way of thinking. Nevertheless, the ideas of earlier thinkers linger on in the consciousness of both groups. Neither French nor English in Canada seem able to accept the idea of a blend of the two cultures. This encourages polarization of the two groups and the continuation of unhealthy political problems wherever they are forced to live together.

Francophones in Ontario are forced to be hybrids if they want to keep their French heritage and still participate in an English society. Culturally, however, they are often treated as pariahs and rejected by both English and French. Many of the French in Quebec see bicultural francophones from Ontario not only as tarnished but also as a threat. On the other hand, the English in Ontario often suspect Franco-Ontarians of favouring independence for Quebec, and therefore question their loyalty to Canada. Because of these reactions, many Franco-Ontarians feel they must choose between one camp or the other—so they move to Montreal and live exclusively in French, or go to Toronto and immerse themselves in English culture.

In spite of all the obstacles, a growing number of individuals are learning how to benefit from these two cultural worlds, which so many consider to be irreconcilable. The most striking example is that of businessman Paul Desmarais, who in 1960 left Sudbury for Ottawa and later Montreal. For many years, certain Quebec intellectuals portrayed him as an outsider with undesirable capitalistic and "English" characteristics. Gradually, Desmarais shed this image; now his success is largely attributed to his capacity to move in the two cultures as no other Canadian businessman has been able to do before him.

The cultural dilemma of the Franco-Ontarians characterizes in the most poignant way the central problem of Canada. The conflict between English and French in Canada has been marked by an ongoing tug of war over language use—from the Proclamation of Quebec in 1763 to Regulation 17, the Royal Commission on Bilingualism and Biculturalism, and Quebec's Bill 101. The way in which francophones in Ontario are struggling to reconcile the divergent demands of the two key cultural elements of Canadian society is the subject of this book.

Part I

The Quiet Revolution in Nouvel-Ontario

In the early 1970s Nouvel-Ontario experienced a Quiet Revolution that transformed the attitudes of people in the region. The changes that took place were inspired by the new spirit in Quebec, but they were of a different order. Because Franco-Ontarians could not become a separate nation or even an autonomous society, they never expressed the desire for a different role for the state. The heroes of the Quiet Revolution in Nouvel-Ontario, therefore, did not leave their mark in politics. What interested them most was culture, business, and everyday social activities.

As in Quebec, there were two phases to the Quiet Revolution that unfolded in Nouvel-Ontario. The first was an intense blossoming of plays, poetry, and music as the French community started to anxiously question its cultural destiny. Later, during a second phase, people suddenly became aware of the economic dimension of society. A group of businessmen, entrepreneurs, and people involved in the co-operative movement urged the community to establish more French economic institutions as it shifted from a rural to an industrial society. They saw this as an essential condition for the preservation of French culture in Ontario.

It was the artists that first helped the people of Nouvel-Ontario see their culture in a new light. At the heart of the outpouring of activity in theatre, music, and poetry was André Paiement and a commune of young writers and performers who created the Coopérative des Artistes du Nouvel-Ontario (CANO) in Sudbury in 1972. For minorities with a will to flourish, the performing arts are often their only means of self-expression. Welsh poet Mervyn Peake wrote of his homeland: "The Celtic bird that has no wing ... Only song, that indestructible that golden thing." Blacks in the United States understood this well: when life with the majority became intolerable, they turned to the stage to express themselves.

The flowering of theatre in Sudbury in the early 1970s was a response to the breakdown of traditional values and life-styles in Nouvel-Ontario. The institutions of the rural parish offered city dwellers no protection against the encroachments of industry and the consumer society. People who had moved from the country to the city felt alienated because the French language seemed to have no place in their new environment. The spectre of assimilation hovered over them. To preserve their collective sanity and heritage, the young artists tried to capture the essence of their culture in art.

It was not until several years later that the French in Ontario shifted their attention to the economy. In fact, the Quiet Revolution in Ontario is still going on as Franco-Ontarians continue to try to come to terms in a practical way with the realities of industrial society. In this respect, the work of French businessmen and activists in the co-operative movement will be as instrumental to the future of Nouvel-Ontario as the plays and music of its artists; for without a larger economic infrastructure, the French in Ontario run the risk of becoming little more than an ethnic group.

Chapter 2

Mon pays

My flour mill
My village
My three friends
My two languages
When my country was just a landscape
Lively
Ageless

The sounding bell
Doesn't tell our song
It finds courage in distance
Because today with no compass to steer by
We sail with grappling hooks at the ready

André Paiement, song from a CANO album, 1977[1]

The Cultural Explosion

The weekly drama class at École secondaire Macdonald-Cartier, Sudbury's largest French high school, was about to start. Pre-performance jitters were in the air as the students tumbled in carrying copies of *Les vieux m'ont conté*, a series of Franco-Ontarian folk tales gathered over thirty years by the Sudbury folklorist, Père Germain Lemieux.[2] Five students would be reciting from Lemieux's collection for the class. "*C'est ton tour, n'est-ce-pas?*" a student asked Sylvie Thibeault, who was going over her lines. "*Tu n'es pas nerveuse?*" "*Non,*" Sylvie replied, "*juste excitée.*"

For these francophone students, the theatre is an exciting milieu where they have proved they are superior to their English peers. The notice board was cluttered with photographs from prize-winning plays written by students for the annual provincial drama festival. Posters of plays from the local French theatre house covered the walls. One poster advertised *La tante*, a play by former student Robert Marinier, now a professional actor and playwright. A huge cartoon served as a stage backdrop for the classroom: it showed a youth on a stool, holding a brush, with a can on his head marked *binnes*. Underneath were the words: "*Au jeune théâtre, par la magie de la transposition, un tabouret devient un trône, une boite de conserve une couronne, une brosse un sceptre.*" In youth theatre, by the magic of transposition, a stool becomes a throne, a can of preserves, a crown, and a brush, a sceptre.

Straddling a chair at the front of the class, Sylvie announced: "The folk tale I will recount is called *Le loup et le tonneau*. It was told to Père Lemieux in St. Charles, Ontario, by Wilfrid Viau, who heard it from Ben Levert in 1920 in Sturgeon Falls." Lemieux's stories have a certain magic, and Sylvie's rendition did them justice. She began: "*Enn' foi, c'était en jeune homm' qui s'en allè' au chantier, avait son bagage avec lui, et pui' i' était pas seul: i'y avait t'oûs aut' avec lui ...*" The young audience sat riveted, listening intently to this story about the days of their fathers and grandfathers ... about farmers and loggers and miners ... about Nouvel-Ontario. Continuing in the language of the raconteur, Sylvie told the tale of a lumberjack who got lost in the woods and, after encountering hostile Indians, was miraculously saved by a wolf.

In the four French high schools in the Sudbury area, theatre is an important part of the curriculum. Through plays, skits, and monologues written by Franco-Ontarians, students are developing a deeper awareness of their cultural identity. Unlike the students in Ontario's English schools, they often write their own plays and do it with such aplomb that they have become well known in educational circles across Ontario.

Students in French high schools throughout Ontario have always been encouraged to write their own material. Theatre coach Hélène Gravel first adopted this approach when Macdonald-Cartier school opened in 1969. At province-wide conferences on education, teachers from English schools were amazed at what she was able to achieve. "They'd like to be able to do the same thing," said Gravel. "But they can't imagine where they'd even start. I've explained that for us it's a matter of necessity. There are not enough suitable plays for our students to perform. That's the way it is for minorities like us. To survive we must create our own things—so we do. It's as simple as that. Students are capable of writing their own plays. Once you convince them of that they can sit down and write."

On the outskirts of Sudbury, in the French town of Azilda, students were rehearsing a musical production at École secondaire Rayside. The cafeteria, transformed into a steamy *boîte à musique*, exploded with live French rock music from Sudbury, Montreal, and Paris. One of the songs was from *La vie et les temps de Médéric Boileau*, a rock opera by the late playwright and musician, André Paiement, about a lumberjack who has spent his life in isolated lumber camps in northern Ontario and retires to the strange town of Sudbury. Dressed in overalls and a battered hunting jacket, student Gilles Simon played the role of the bewildered *vieux Médé* while a rock combo and a girls' chorus led by Line Roberge belted out:

Old Médéric
has just come out of the woods
And I have a feeling
that he's lost

For the love of St-Pierre de Porquépique
and St-Herménégilde
Poor old Médéric Boileau
has just hit town
. . . .

Fifty years in the woods —
Can you imagine?
It sure won't be easy
for an old codger like him
To make it in the big city.[3]

After the instruments and the sound system had been packed up, Gilles and Line sat down to tell me about their theatrical ambitions. "We will eventually go to Quebec to study, but we can do a lot here now," said Gilles. "Our drama teacher, Lise Loiselle, has taught us a lot." Sensitive to any suggestion that Franco-Ontarians did not have an adequate cultural life, they stressed the quality of their French activities. "We have full lives in French. Assimilation is not inevitable," said Line.

Gilles and Line both live in Chelmsford, which is mostly French. Some communities on the outskirts of the city are more French than Sudbury, but even here the French feel under pressure from the English. "There is tension between the two groups," Line admitted. "The English kids I know aren't learning any French. When an English kid comes along we all switch to English."

Like most Franco-Ontarian students at Rayside school, Gilles and Line feel it is important to live in their own cultural world. Both worked during the summer with a province-wide French theatre program called Theâtre-Action, which helps small groups create original plays based on local Franco-Ontarian life and encourages the development of new theatre troupes. Gilles worked in Sturgeon Falls, at an old people's home called Le Chateau where the predominantly female residents wrote a play about their biggest complaint in life: the lack of men. The play, called *La séduction d'Hormidas*, toured church basements and old people's homes in North Bay, Verner, Cache Bay, and Sudbury. Along with some other students, Gilles and Line also wrote a one-act play called *La vie à Chelmsford*, which they presented to their school. Eager to compare notes with other high school theatre groups from Nouvel-Ontario, Gilles later organized a weekend of theatre productions and workshops in Sudbury.

Sylvie, Gilles, and Line are part of a new generation in Nouvel-Ontario who regard participation in French theatre and other cultural activities as natural. This generation is the embryo of a new middle class essential for the development of Franco-Ontarian society in the 1980s. In the past, Nouvel-Ontario consisted of closed communities of farmers, lumberjacks, and miners, with a small elite of teachers and clergy led by the Jesuits. There was no real middle class. The community resisted assimilation mainly because it was isolated from the main currents of English urban and industrial life. Since the early 1960s, however, all this has changed. Nouvel-Ontario is now poised between a traditional rural mentality and an urban industrial consciousness, just as Quebec was in the 1950s. It needs a vibrant middle class with its own theatre, music, art, radio, and other institutions to help it make the rapid transition from one type of society to another.

This middle class is being created by the French public high schools which opened in Nouvel-Ontario in 1969 after the province passed new laws governing French education. Until then, only the elite could afford to send their children to the Jesuits' Collège du Sacré-Cœur or the Oblate's University of Ottawa; the rest never got beyond elementary school. Some of the less affluent tried to educate their children in what the French Catholic priests called "the godless English schools," but most students entered with minimal English and became so discouraged they soon dropped out. Now the children of French working-class families are finishing high school, looking forward to careers in a variety of fields, and developing middle-class habits, tastes, and ambitions.

Hopes for the future of Nouvel-Ontario rest with this new generation, according to Hector Bertrand, editor of the weekly *Le Voyageur* in Sudbury. "For the size of our community, we should have a daily paper," he said. "We don't have one because the middle class is too small and underdeveloped. If no new middle class rises up to support French cultural institutions such as newspapers, theatre, and art galleries, assimilation will be inevitable."

The year 1969—when French public high schools opened in Ontario—was a turning point for Sudbury. No one recognized it at the time, but it marked the beginning of the Quiet Revolution that triggered an unprecedented explosion of cultural activity. Artistic developments took two distinct directions, reflecting different visions of society. One route was carved out by some young writers, poets, and musicians who first met at Collège du Sacré-Coeur in the early sixties and later reunited at Laurentian University. They founded the Théâtre du Nouvel-Ontario in 1970 and, led by Paiement, created experimental rock musicals. Their work reflected the frantic search for identity going on among the generation of educated francophones brought up in the sixties who found themselves midway between the death of traditional Nouvel-Ontario and the birth of nationalist Quebec.

The other cultural route was paved in the seventies by Hélène Gravel, who later became a special consultant for the French schools in Ontario. A graduate of Laurentian University's French teaching college, she was hired by École secondaire Macdonald-Cartier when it first opened to work with students who were interested in drama. Although she had no formal theatrical training, Gravel helped aspiring actors and writers win first prizes at the prestigious Simpson-Sears Ontarian Collegiate Drama Festival, competing with the best English troupes in Ontario. A number of her protégés were accepted by the National Theatre School in Montreal and are now professional actors and writers. Unlike the Paiement generation, Gravel's students were much more willing to accept a bicultural identity. Many were the children of miners who had already come to terms with English and French in their daily lives. Growing up in the seventies, they were more preoccupied with personal development than with collective identity.

The members of the Théâtre du Nouvel-Ontario, on the other hand, were part of the idealistic generation of the sixties that believed in radical social change. The children of the middle-class elite, they were among the last of the privileged youth to come under the influence of the Jesuits who ran the Collège du Sacré-Cœur. Because of their traditional and classical education, they believed French culture in Ontario should be kept pure. As Quebec's nationalist movement gained momentum, they looked for a way to create as extensive a French cultural base in Ontario as possible.

Robert Marinier, a professional actor and playwright who shuttles between Sudbury, Ottawa, and Montreal, is one of a half-dozen successful artists who started with Gravel. Tall and supple, with a quizzical expression and wide, brown eyes, Marinier looks like a young French harlequin. But he has an English side as well, and switches easily from French to English when talking. Where Paiement was a purist who fought to be like the French in Quebec, Marinier accepts the duality of his identity. Whether he lives in Ontario or Quebec, he will always fall between the two cultural worlds, belonging entirely to neither one nor the other.

Marinier is the son of a French miner who came to Sudbury in the 1950s from Hull, Quebec. Like many graduates of Macdonald-Cartier, Marinier's was the first generation to go to high school. When the school opened in 1969, he was attending an English institution. "My first acting experience was at LaSalle High," he recalled. "It was just by chance that I got a part in a play. They needed a black for *You Can't Take It With You*, but there were no blacks around. The director decided that since I had a French accent, I would do. In those days the French-Canadians were students *de deuxième zone*. We never felt free to speak French with one another around the school, and strange as it may seem, we never really questioned it. So I was the *nègre blanc* in the play. I'd probably do it again," he laughed, "but this time I'd understand what it was all about."

I met Marinier in October 1980, when he was directing his play *La tante* for the Théâtre du Nouvel-Ontario in Sudbury. *La tante* is a comedy about two cousins who are waiting for their old aunt to depart from this world and try to cut each other out of her will. The play contains no anguished exploration of cultural identity like the works of Paiement, but it is unmistakably Franco-Ontarian in language and spirit.

Marinier acquired his taste for French theatre while learning about writing and acting under Gravel. He and his fellow students wrote plays about their everyday lives. *Le jeu de cartes*, the school's first play to win an award, is about two young people who became involved in an encounter group run by a charlatan. Other plays by Gravel's students explore the effects of the media on teenagers and the difficulties of communication between people. "Our mentality was different from the Paiement group," Marinier said. "We were not engaged in a conscious search for identity. But we were very influenced by what the people in the Théâtre du Nouvel-Ontario were doing. I remember seeing the first play, *Moé j'viens du Nord 'stie*. It was in French, it had a rock band, and it was about us! I'd never seen anything like it before. It was part of a reawakening in Sudbury."

After Marinier graduated from Macdonald-Cartier, he enrolled in the National Theatre School in Montreal, where he encountered the French culture of Quebec face to face for the first time. Montreal was not what he expected. "I discovered that I was a foreigner," he said. "I knew nothing of Quebec cultural life—the *chansonniers*, the playwrights, the political situation—it was all new." The French / English mix was also different. Marinier lived in two cultures in Sudbury, but in the artistic milieu that he became part of in Montreal, this was not possible. "I like speaking English," he explained. "It's part of me. It blew my mind to meet French people who couldn't speak a word of English."

Most alarming for Marinier were the complaints he received from the National Theatre School about the quality of his French. Other students from Sudbury who attended the school had the same experience. "When I entered I spoke kitchen French," Marinier said. "I had gone to French school, but only for three years. We weren't exposed to much good French in Sudbury—when I left, the local Radio-Canada station hadn't even opened." To improve his French, he spent a summer back in Sudbury taking French courses at Laurentian University; eventually he was accepted into Montreal theatre circles.

Although he enjoyed living in Quebec, Marinier has kept his Franco-Ontarian attachments and now makes Ottawa his base of operations. After graduating from theatre school in Montreal in 1976, he became artist-in-residence for two years at the Théâtre du Nouvel-Ontario in Sudbury. The highlight of his tenure was his performance in the title role of *Ti-Jean de mon pays*, written by Nicole Beauchamp, a colleague from his days at Macdonald-Cartier high school. Beauchamp based her text upon tales of Ti-Jean taken from Germain Lemieux's collection of folk stories. With Marinier in the lead, the play enjoyed enormous success on a tour of hundreds of cities and villages across Canada in 1977.

In his work, Marinier draws from both of his cultural backgrounds. For two summers he worked in a bilingual theatre troupe composed of young French and English writers and actors from Sudbury. The group toured northern Ontario and the Maritimes, performing what Marinier called "story theatre" for children. "We worked terrifically together in the two languages," he said. "The format we used was fine everywhere except in one town outside Quebec City where the audience objected to the English pieces."

Although a graduate of the National Theatre School, Marinier doesn't consider his way of working particularly French. In his production of *La tante* at the Théâtre du Nouvel-Ontario, for example, he used an English approach in the direction. The actors, who were all from Quebec, found it new. "The style I tried for," he said during a break in rehearsal, "was the same as what you'd find in an Agatha Christie whodunit. Where did I absorb this English style? Well, from television, from my reading, and from going to Stratford."

More than any other element of the Quiet Revolution, the Coopérative des Artistes du Nouvel-Ontario radically changed cultural life in Sudbury. Led by Paiement, the group included theatre director Pierre Bélanger, singer Robert Paquette, and poet Gaston Tremblay. The movement started in 1969 at Laurentian University when a group of writers and artists founded a literary paper, held poetry readings, and began writing multi-media rock dramas. The Théâtre du Nouvel-Ontario and the folk-rock group CANO (now called Masque) exist today because of them.

The people who created these organizations broke with the stifling survivalist philosophy that characterized the older generation of Franco-Ontarians. Ever since Regulation 17 was passed in 1912, the French elite had thought that all it could hope to do was secure the community's position. The Catholic church was its refuge; fighting for French schools its main activity. Paiement's group tried to rise above the restrictive framework imposed by the social and political organization of the traditional parish.

Quebec provided them with an example of what could be accomplished. "We were excited by the artistic activity in Quebec," said Gaston Tremblay, who directs Prise de Parole. "What was going on in Quebec affected us deeply. But Quebec wanted independence—its own territory—and that excluded us." The Franco-Ontarians were ambivalent about the nationalist movement in Quebec. On the one hand they felt abandoned when René Lévesque called them "dead ducks." But at the same time, Quebec's cultural renaissance served as a beacon in their search for their own kind of *francophonie*.

The Americans, however, influenced the Sudbury artists as much as the French in Quebec did. It was the time of *Hair* and student protests and LSD. Tom Wolfe and other American writers were creating "the new journalism" with articles and books inspired by a fresh social perspective. What made the Franco-Ontarians different from their Quebec counterparts was that they were part of this world. They could absorb the sounds and styles of New York and San Francisco in a way that performers in Quebec could not.

Because French performers spoke English effortlessly from childhood, they were "in touch with the rest of North American folk and popular music as few Québécois have ever been," wrote Malcolm Reid in an article on the explosion of French cultural activity outside Quebec. "Charlebois *tried* to assimilate rock, but Monique Paiement of Sturgeon Falls, Ontario, and Patsy Gallant of Campbellton, New Brunswick, *were* rock. Jim and Bertrand from the Eastern Townships tried to bring the gentle American ballad spirit of Simon and Garfunkel into the French language, but Robert Paquette was *born* into the same society as Gordon Lightfoot. He had integrated this tradition deep down at his musical core."[4]

The music of young Franco-Ontarians like Robert Paquette reflects many influences—the Scottish ballad, Kentucky bluegrass, and American hard rock, as well as the French folk songs of their fathers and grandfathers. What pushed them to create, however, was the search for a new cultural identity. This was what the Théâtre du Nouvel-Ontario was all about. Their *pays*, or homeland, was in ferment and the question everyone was asking was this: Would Nouvel-Ontario be able to transform itself?

From 1970 to 1975 the Théâtre du Nouvel-Ontario produced five major works by Paiement, with music and songs by Robert Paquette, Marcel Aymar, and others. During this time the group operated as a co-operative that moved from the campus of Laurentian University to a buffalo ranch some eighty kilometres away in Earlton to the basement of St. Anne's church in Sudbury and finally to the *La Slague* theatre house. The productions usually opened in Sudbury and then toured Nouvel-Ontario.

The French in Sudbury reacted to Paiement and his group in different ways. For the traditional leadership of the community, the new theatre was a scandal. The group's anti-clerical attitudes, its marijuana parties, and its use of *joual*[5] French was disturbing. It was as if Sudbury had been invaded by a clan of Michel Tremblays. The group was too avant-garde for much of the community, but it had a substantial following among the French students.

Paquette, a *chansonnier* who later moved to Montreal, remembers how the first production, Moé j'viens du Nord 'stie, was received when it toured the north in 1970. "We had put up posters all over, but when we arrived in Kapuskasing, we found the priests had taken them down and had told everyone to stay away. They didn't like the fact that the play was in the ordinary language of the people and contained swearing. We went on radio and invited the whole town to a free concert at six o'clock. When people came, we told them that at nine we were offering Moé j'viens du Nord 'stie."

The play is about a youth torn between university and the quick money of the mines and sawmills. "We used colour slides as a backdrop," he recalled. "When we arrived in each town, we'd take new slides and use them in the production. Also, we changed the script to give it local colour—we talked about mining in mining towns, and the sawmill in lumbering towns. When people saw it they said: 'Hey, can you believe it, that's us!' For the first time Franco-Ontarians were seeing themselves in a play. It was a tremendous cultural event—a hit! Young people could relate to it even if the church could not."

Cultural life in the English community of Sudbury was quiet, so some anglophone intellectuals joined Paiement's group. Robert Dickson, who went to Sudbury in the early seventies to teach French-Canadian literature at Laurentian University, was one of them. Originally from southern Ontario, Dickson had studied at Laval University in Quebec City where he had become so immersed in Quebec culture that he started to write poetry in French. Dickson introduced some of his students in Sudbury to Montreal poet Gaston Miron, who still takes an interest in Franco-Ontarian writers. A member of the Coopérative des Artists du Nouvel-Ontario, Dickson helped found Prise de Parole with fellow poet Gaston Tremblay and is still active in Franco-Ontarian literary and theatre circles.

Mick Lowe, who went on to become a radio playwright and a labour reporter for the *Globe and Mail*, was another sympathizer. A draft dodger who left the United States in 1970, he breezed into Sudbury in 1974 from Vancouver. "I remember meeting Suzie Beauchemin, the actress and girl friend of André Paiement," he said. "I saw her in a restaurant and found her mesmerizing, so I followed her into the basement of St. Anne's church where the Théâtre du Nouvel-Ontario was rehearsing. I wanted to know what the people in the group were all about. She explained that first and foremost they were not Québécois. Later I saw her in *Lavalléville*. After that I started to learn French and to go to their parties. *Lavalléville* was a brilliant rock opera. Suzie Beauchemin was a truly great performer. If she had lived, she could have made it big in Montreal and Paris."

The theatre pieces of Paiement and his colleagues were exciting and imaginative but their themes were dark and murky. *Moé j'viens du Nord 'stie* is about a miner's son who is too demoralized to escape from his background. *Lavalléville* takes its inspiration from an isolated French sawmill village called Dubreuilville, in the heart of the forest near Wawa. Run by the Dubreuil brothers, the town was closed off for many years from the outside world; the play examines the perils of being too inward-looking. Paiement's *À mes fils bien-aimés* is about fratricide and hints at a death wish which seemed to be part of his despair about himself and his culture. Drugs and hype and a recklessness that went with rock music were part of the ambiance of the Théâtre du Nouvel-Ontario group. *Et le septième jour* tells of the last week of a speed freak. Many members of the group went on to pursue stable lives, but Beauchemin and Paiement came to tragic ends. She died in a car crash while still in her twenties; he committed suicide in Sudbury in 1978.

The gloominess of the young artists' themes, however, was alleviated by their celebration of northern living. The play that most beautifully captures the sense of the north is *La vie et les temps de Médéric Boileau*: a hymn to the joys of the woods and winter, of warmth around the hearth, of strong friendships and old traditions — of being French Canadian.

> Winter evenings here
> were quiet and peaceful
> nothing to do but sit and listen
> to the snoring of the old
> pot-bellied stove
> that kept us warm.
>
> Yes, winter was always
> what I liked the best.[6]

But the hymn is also nostalgic and sad. Médéric Boileau represents a people who cling to their traditions in the face of assimilation. His story is about the passing of an era and the beginning of a time of confusion.

Quebec literature in the early days of the Quiet Revolution reflected completely different concerns. Poets longed for their own country, spiritually and politically. In the early sixties, the fact that this objective had not been realized was experienced as a wound. Jean-Guy Pilon's poem "Je murmure le nom de mon pays" reflects this feeling:

> I whisper my country's name
> softly to myself
> like an obscene secret,
> or a hidden wound in my soul.
> And I no longer know
> where the winds come from
> or where her borders are
> or where her cities start

The poem ends with this prophecy:

> But one morning
> Like a child at the end of a long journey
> we'll stretch out our arms
> in a country that will welcome us
> its name given without shame
> no longer murmured
> but proclaimed.[7]

Later, Quebec poets such as Paul Chamberland became still more politicized.

Unlike the French in Quebec, Franco-Ontarians could not imagine moving from patriotism and regionalism to a concrete political goal. This explains why the Franco-Ontarians are so pre-occupied with biculturalism, with all its painful problems. A recurrent theme of many of Paiement's pieces—in fact, in most modern Franco-Ontarian literature—is the divided self. Gaston Tremblay, a close friend of Paiement, saw the people in *La vie et les temps de Médéric Boileau* as suffering from the tension of two languages and two cultures, of city versus country—and even of life and death.

After 1975, the people most active in the Théâtre du Nouvel-Ontario and the Coopérative des Artistes du Nouvel-Ontario started to look beyond Sudbury and the north. The mass audiences of Montreal and Toronto beckoned. Paquette eventually established himself in Montreal, while Paiement threw his energies into CANO-Musique, as it was then called, a bilingual folk-rock group which moved to Toronto in the early eighties.

The Théâtre du Nouvel-Ontario took on a new image after Paiement resigned as director in 1975. Hélène Gravel, who was in charge of drama at Macdonald-Cartier high school, took over and the theatre became less controversial and more acceptable to ordinary people. The theatre continued to present original works by Franco-Ontarian writers, but it also offered standard theatre repertoire and created a theatre program for students in co-operation with local high schools.

By 1981 French theatre in Sudbury was nowhere near as vital as it was in the early seventies. The hub of Franco-Ontarian theatre had, in fact, shifted to the eastern region of the province with the birth in the mid-1970s of groups such as La Corvée in Ottawa and the Théâtre d'la Veille 17 in Rockland. To help the Théâtre du Nouvel-Ontario regain its position, poet and actor Jean-Marc Dalpé and theatre director Brigitte Haentjens, who were instrumental in developing theatre in the east, came to Sudbury in 1982. Under them, the theatre once again became a touring company presenting new works by Franco-Ontarian writers. Along with his work at the Théâtre du Nouvel-Ontario, Dalpé is setting up new programs to stimulate more amateur theatre in Sudbury. "Eventually the Théâtre du Nouvel-Ontario should rest with people who live here in the region," he said. "This can only be done if we develop more theatrical talent in the community."

CANO-Musique is the only French folk-rock group from the diaspora that has become popular with young people in Quebec. The lament for the passing of a traditional society in a song such as Paiement's Mon pays strikes a sympathetic chord in Quebec.

My flour mill
My village
My three friends
My two languages
When my country was just a landscape
Lively
Ageless

The sounding bell
Doesn't tell our song
It finds courage in distance
Because today with no compass to steer by
We sail with grappling hooks at the ready.

Other songs — Au nord de notre vie, for example, which captures the spirit of Nouvel-Ontario with its snows and wild life, its lumber camps and mines — give CANO's music regional character that is equally appealing.

From the beginning, CANO-Musique sang and worked in French and English. But when Paiement died, the French component of the group lost its force. Its records sold well in Quebec, but it did not have a large enough French repertoire to visit Quebec on a regular basis. CANO-Musique finally decided to become an English group after it discovered that Quebec audiences would not accept a blend of French and English songs. When the band went to Montreal in 1978 after Paiement's death, it was booed for singing in English. CANO-Musique was primarily French, but from the beginning the group billed itself as a mixture of many cultures. On the jacket of its album *Tous dans le même bateau*, the group explained that its members were Franco-Ontarian, Acadian, English, and Ukrainian, and that its lyrics and music reflected many ethnic origins. The French presence in CANO-Musique remained after Paiement died, but the group quickly realized it was not French enough for Quebec. In 1981 it changed its name to Masque and began singing almost exclusively in English, hoping to break into the American market.

Paquette has created a solid following for himself both in and outside Quebec. He now gives over one hundred concerts a year — more than most Quebec performers. Though he still considers Nouvel-Ontario his home, he moved to Montreal for professional reasons. "Franco-Ontarians are marginal and will always be so," he explained. "We don't have a strong enough collectivity to support us, so we must leave and 'make it' as individuals."

Because of this marginality, Paquette has absorbed a variety of cultural influences and created a style that appeals to a broad audience. He is popular not only in Sudbury and northern Ontario, but also in Quebec, English Canada, the eastern United States, and Europe. Paquette was forced to diversify because he is not from Quebec and cannot command the same support there as a *pure laine*—a francophone with deep Quebec roots. "Let's face it," he said. "When I perform I'm not a cultural event. Since I'm not from Quebec, I can't be politically *engagé*." Like the members of many minority groups, Paquette feels as though he is from nowhere and everywhere. "I am not really a Quebec musician because I'm on the road ten months a year. But I'm not really a Franco-Ontarian musician either. *"Je suis à part. Je suis toujours le marginal, à côté, mais totalement présent.* I stand apart, I am always on the margins, always to one side, but very present. *C'est une ambivalence qui vient avec la naissance.* It's an ambivalence that comes with birth: *positif, négatif, le ying, le yang, le chaud, le froid, mâle, femelle, la relativité des choses forme ma constante.*"

Paquette sometimes sings in English, but he is essentially a French *chansonnier* who wins over audiences across Canada even when he sings in his mother tongue. Young anglophones out West, for example, warm to his French songs even though they can't always follow the lyrics. His records, all of them in French, sell especially well in Quebec and in French communities across Canada. He is one of a growing number of francophone performers from outside Quebec, including Edith Butler, Patsy Gallant, and Angèle Arseneault, who regularly perform at festivals mounted by the French communities outside Quebec.

Paquette returns to his native Sudbury and the north almost every year and his concerts are always treated as special events. Nevertheless, he feels nervous in his home town. "I never know how I'm going to be treated when I go home. I was the first singer there to make it, and they're inclined to be critical. They're always testing to see whether I'm still one of them."

An important ingredient of the cultural revolution in northern Ontario was the expansion of Prise de Parole publishing house. Inspired by the example of l'Hexagone, established in Montreal by poet Gaston Miron, Prise de Parole was set up to encourage and publish Franco-Ontarian writers. Launched on a shoe-string budget in 1973, it quickly grew to a full-time operation with the help of the French section of the Ontario Arts Council. Its first title was an anthology of Franco-Ontarian poetry called *Lignes-Signes*; since then it has published more than thirty books, including plays, novels, biographies, and even school texts. Since 1980, the reputation of Prise de Parole has spread beyond Franco-Ontario to Quebec and the French communities across Canada. Paiement's plays, illustrated by Sudbury artist Luc Robert, have been compared by critics to those of Quebec's Michel Tremblay. *La parole et la loi*, written collectively by a group called La Corvée and dealing with Regulation 17, has also been well received. The most controversial of Prise de Parole's recent publications, however, promises to be a long prose-poem in French and English by Timmins writer Patrice Desbiens. Called *L'homme invisible / The Invisible Man*, it explores the uncertain universe of the bicultural personality.

Where has the Quiet Revolution in cultural activity left Nouvel-Ontario today? Part of the answer lies in the attitudes of young people such as Sylvie Thibeault, Gilles Simon, and Line Roberge. They are more sure of their Nouvel-Ontario identity than previous generations who had no French high schools and few cultural institutions at their disposal. Because of the presence of the Théâtre du Nouvel-Ontario and Prise de Parole, for example, young francophones who are interested in careers in the arts have successful Franco-Ontarian models to follow. The experiences of Hélène Gravel, Robert Marinier, Gaston Tremblay, and many others demonstrate that Franco-Ontarians can excel in a contemporary world. Cultural activities are no longer confined to songs and stories around the hearth.

It is too early to assess the permanent effects of the cultural revolution upon Nouvel-Ontario. The middle class that is necessary to support the spread of new cultural values has not yet developed sufficiently. There is no French book store or daily French newspaper in Sudbury. All of Prise de Parole's books are sold by mail order or through the schools and universities. The cultural revolution of the seventies definitely changed life in Sudbury. It remains to be seen whether the generation of the eighties can sustain the momentum of creative activity started by André Paiement and the Coopérative des Artistes du Nouvel-Ontario.

Chapter 3

There will be hope for Canadian unity only when French Canadians break into business the way Paul Desmarais has.

Gaston Demers, stockbroker, Sudbury

If we don't develop some kind of economic infrastructure in French, we will become folklorized and nothing more than an ethnic group.

Gérard Lafrenière, director,
Études en coopératisme,
Laurentian University, Sudbury

The French Fact
in the Economy

Timmins-born broadcasting magnate Conrad Lavigne is a man who doesn't take no for an answer. In 1950 he started the first French radio station in Ontario, largely because he was angry at an English station. At the time, Lavigne was running a small hotel in Kirkland Lake. Once a week he and a group of friends produced a French show for the local English radio station. They told jokes, sang songs, and did one-act plays—all in French. "It was a popular program," he said, "and we had a lot of listeners. But one day the manager of the station came in and told us that he'd had it. He was fed up running a French program on his English station and he was cutting us off—just like that!

"There was no way I was going to take that lying down. I was used to dealing with anti-French feelings, but this sort of arrogance was too much—so I made up my mind to start a station of my own. There were no French radio stations in Ontario, and I knew nothing about the broadcasting business. But I didn't let that stop me," he laughed. "I decided to apply to the authorities for a station in Timmins." Lavigne had worked in the city as a butcher before the war, so he knew the place well. He spent a year preparing a document that justified the need for a French radio station in the north. "It was a tremendous effort, but I won," he said with a grin.

From that one French radio station, Lavigne built up a radio and television network in both French and English serving north-eastern Ontario, part of Quebec, and the Ottawa valley. When he sold his holdings in 1980, his company, Mid-Canada Television, served over 250,000 square miles.

Lavigne prided himself on learning everything about the nuts and bolts of the broadcasting business, including how to build television relay stations. Lithe and handsome, with an old-fashioned charm, he looks like an aristocrat. Yet when there was manual work to be done, he poured cement and wielded a pick and shovel.

Conrad Lavigne and other French businessmen in Nouvel-Ontario have regarded business as a kind of game, full of risks but offering the chance to build an empire. However, they have worked alone, with little support from their community, because the traditional elite was convinced that industrial and capitalist society threatened French and Catholic values.

When Lavigne set out to build his empire, the self-contained rural parish was already disintegrating. Yet the majority of the French still hesitated to venture into the world of business. Consequently, the French language had no status in the day-to-day activities of a place like Timmins, even though the city had a large French population. People such as Conrad Lavigne left French at the doors of their homes like comfortable slippers when they went out into the entrepreneurial world. "English was the language of business. That was something we accepted," he said.

Since the early 1950s, Conrad Lavigne has been active in every important Franco-Ontarian institution, from the *caisses populaires* to the French section of Laurentian University. He considers himself to be very French. Yet in the 1950s and 1960s, when he was building his broadcasting empire, he accepted the idea that the French language would never occupy a significant place in public life.

The difficulty in questioning this state of affairs is illustrated by an incident involving a Quebec priest who went to Timmins in 1960 to head one of the French parishes. Shortly after his arrival, the priest tried to make some local telephone calls in French. Since there was no personal dialing, all calls went through a central switchboard. Timmins had a large French community, but the priest soon discovered that none of the operators could speak French. Outraged, he decided to force the issue.

He went to every French elementary school in the city and persuaded the children to bombard the operators with French calls. In two days the children had paralysed the entire Timmins phone system: businessmen were in an uproar, firemen were the last to learn of fires—and the priest seemed well on the way to winning. To his great surprise, just when it seemed that the phone company might have to provide a service in French, Lavigne intervened. In an emotional personal appearance on his own French radio station, he appealed to parents to pry their children away from the phones and abandon the priest's scheme. "I had to do something," he recalled. "Luckily, it all died down in a hurry."

Lavigne felt that the phone company was wrong to have a unilingual policy, but that the priest's action went too far. In his view, the behaviour of the priest went against the kind of accommodations that the French and English had worked out in the region. "Such aggressive conduct," he concluded, "would have led to bad blood between the two groups." The priest, no longer welcome in Timmins, met a fate similar to that of Monseigneur Charbonneau, the archbishop of Montreal who was exiled to western Canada at the instigation of Premier Duplessis for supporting the 1949 strike by Quebec asbestos workers. "We made some sort of arrangements for him," said Lavigne with a smile. "I think he went somewhere in Africa."

Although this first generation of francophone businessmen judged that the times were not propitious to fight for a greater role for French in Nouvel-Ontario, younger Franco-Ontarians have worked to expand the place of French in all domains, including business and commerce. Several factors contributed to this shift in perspective: the acceptance of official bilingualism by the federal government in 1969, the rise of nationalism in Quebec, and changes in the attitudes of the French in Quebec concerning their participation in economic life.

In the mid-1960s, when the head offices of large Canadian corporations started leaving Montreal for Ontario and the West, many predicted that Quebec would become an economic backwater. Montreal has suffered from the displacement of North American economic activity toward the centre of the continent and the Pacific coast. But the city's economic life is being renewed as a result of the unexpected vitality of French society in Quebec.

Montreal is giving birth to a second national economy, with French as its principal language and branches reaching across Canada.

In the wake of the Quiet Revolution, a new class of business-men, entrepreneurs, and senior civil servants has emerged in Quebec. With the consolidation of assets by the Fédération des caisses populaires Desjardins and the Banque nationale, the appearance of conglomerates like Power Corporation, the expansion of crown corporations like Hydro-Quebec and Sidbec, and the enterprising spirit of firms like Bombardier and Quebecor, French society in Quebec has acquired a new economic dimension. Those who contributed to it—Alfred Rouleau, Paul Desmarais, and Michel Bélanger, among others—have enlarged the range of influence of the French language and provided new models for successive generations. The psychological effect of this development is felt not only in Quebec but across the country, and especially in Nouvel-Ontario. Lavigne conceived of success in English terms, but younger Franco-Ontarians, having witnessed the changes in Quebec, now think differently.

More and more francophone businessmen in Sudbury believe that Nouvel-Ontario must develop some economic institutions of its own if the region is to survive the transition from a rural to an industrial economy. They can see that young people are not using enough French in their training and work to keep the language rich. "If we are to survive," said historian Gaétan Gervais, a professor at Laurentian University, "we must develop some economic organizations in French." The push for more participation in the economy is now a priority for many francophone communities across Canada. In the spring of 1982, the Fédération des francophones hors Québec held a national conference to stimulate an exchange of ideas on the topic.

To tackle the problem in Sudbury, a new generation of Nouvel-Ontario businessmen and entrepreneurs are actively promoting the use of French in commerce. These people do not have many institutional tools at their disposal. For example, in 1982 business administration programs at Laurentian University were still available only in English. However, through their personal example, the new generation of businessmen is making people aware that French need not be confined to the private world of home, church, and cultural activities.

Gaston Demers was the only French stockbroker in Sudbury on the day the 1980 federal budget was to be announced. He was on the phone to his clients at Pitfield Mackay Ross, talking excitedly in French. "I'm recommending Petrofina," he said to one of them. "The government is expected to announce the new energy policy — through Petro Canada, it will try to buy up an oil company. I've been doing some research," he said, "and I figure it will be Petrofina. To take it over, the government will be prepared to pay at least 50 per cent more for the stock. It looks like the government wants to create a truly Canadian oil company — with outlets from coast to coast."

It was one of my first days in Sudbury and Demers had invited me to lunch with Jean-Noël Desmarais, pillar of the French community and father of Paul Desmarais, Canada's leading francophone businessman. As we settled into lunch at the Peter Piper restaurant, Demers discussed his Petrofina theory with Desmarais. Later, I went back to Demers's office; as the day wore on, it became clear that his speculations had swept through the French community.

Throughout the afternoon a parade of people streamed into his office. One of them was Dan Brophy, a Quebecer of French and Irish descent who teaches at Cambrian College, a bilingual technical institute. "I started investing with Gaston in the stock market a year ago," he said. "He's good for people who know nothing about stocks. He explains everything and he doesn't mind if you have only at little to invest. I come in here every Tuesday. It's one of the highlights of my week."

Like a circus juggler, Demers, dressed casually in corduroy pants and a turtle-neck sweater, took calls, put in requests for stock, and assessed portfolios in French and English, depending upon the client. In between tasks, he nipped across the street to Woolworth's to buy coffee and brownies for his visitors. An excitement akin to the race track gripped his office. Economic studies, the financial pages of *La Presse* and the *Globe and Mail*, and English and French reports from various companies were piled everywhere, but the atmosphere did not correspond to my image of a brokerage office. Not that I had ever been inside such a place until I stepped into number 7, Durham Street, Sudbury. My financial sophistication runs along the lines of the fellow in Stephen Leacock's *My Financial Career* who tiptoes into one of the august St. James Street banks in Montreal to open a savings account and is so intimidated by the apparent financial mumbo-jumbo that he flees before depositing his money.

Demers, however, makes the stock market accessible to people who know nothing about corporations. Since 1976 he has built up an enviable clientele among Sudbury francophones who have never before invested in the stock market. Much of the secret of his success is the confidence he inspires: his hunch about Petrofina, for example, turned out to be right—the federal government bought the company and its stocks jumped 50 per cent.

Before becoming a stockbroker, Demers was the Conservative member of the Ontario legislature for Nickel Belt, in Sudbury. After losing his seat, he invested in an insurance company, bought land for development, and managed the City Centre in Sudbury. "But I was at loose ends," he said. "I had little formal education beyond high school—and I didn't know what to do." So he took an apprenticeship training course at Pitfield Mackay Ross brokerage house. Within a few years he was, as he puts it, "making more money than my old boss, Premier Bill Davis."

The oldest of fifteen children, Demers was brought up on a farm in Verner. His parents could not afford to send him to Collège du Sacré-Coeur for his secondary-level education so, to the disapproval of the local priest, he and a few friends went off to "the godless English high school" in Sturgeon Falls. "I remember that it took us quite some time to learn English," he said. "On the school bus, we used to joke that we had learned how to say yes and no, but we still didn't know *when* to say it." Soon he was fluent enough to write a column on Verner for the *North Bay Nugget* and sell advertising for the newspaper on the side. These English activities were frowned upon by the priest, who did not want his parishioners integrating into the universe of *les autres*. But for Demers, the job was a means of survival. In addition, it introduced him to an exciting world beyond the small French parish of his childhood.

To the tremendous enthusiasm Demers has shown for business—whether buying stocks, developing a shopping centre, or trading in Canadian art—he has added another major concern: the defence of French rights in Ontario. When parents in Penetanguishene were fighting for a separate French high school, he joined the provincial executive of the Association canadienne-française de l'Ontario and pressed their case. When he visited the independent

École de la Huronie, which the parents of Penetanguishene had set up, he took his daughters with him so they could learn at first hand what other young Ontarians were doing to preserve their French culture. And when the Council for Canadian Unity, of which he was a member, refused to take a stand in support of the French parents of Penetanguishene, he wrote an impassioned letter to Bette Stephenson, the Ontario minister of education. "In the current context of a perilous moment in our history as a country," he wrote, "in 1979, Penetanguishene is an incomprehensible chapter in the history of a country which seems bent on committing suicide."

Demers believes that the most efficient way for the French community to improve its situation is to participate more in its economic life. "There will be hope for Canadian unity," he said, "only when French Canadians break into business the way Paul Desmarais has." Demers admits that francophones in Ontario must speak fluent English, but he believes that a significant proportion of business activity can take place in French. "I spend about a quarter of my day speaking the language. Pitfield Mackay Ross provides French reports from its Montreal office which I can offer to my French-speaking clients here in Sudbury."

Demers has used various methods to try to strengthen the French role in Ontario's economy. In 1981–82, for example, he offered two investment courses in French at Cambrian College in Sudbury. He is also president of a provincial committee on the economy which works under the auspices of the Association canadienne-française de l'Ontario. Since 1979 the group has been trying to expand the network of French economic institutions in Ontario by offering professional help to francophone entrepreneurs and holding conferences on topics such as small and medium-sized businesses and the co-operative movement.

Jacques de Courville Nicol, president of a group of electronics companies that operate in both French and English, has been one of the most active businessmen on the ACFO economic committee. While living in Sudbury from 1976 to 1980, he managed the Sudbury division of Conrad Lavigne's Mid-Canada group. When the Lavigne empire was sold, Courville Nicol acquired the electronics division and moved to Ottawa. Called Turnelle, the company has its head office in the federal capital and branches in Ontario and Quebec.

Courville Nicol has spent much of his career trying to improve the status of French outside Quebec. Born in Montreal, but raised in Ottawa, he directed the official languages branch of the federal Treasury Board secretariat which was responsible for implementing bilingualism in the civil service. Now he is trying to encourage francophones to participate more in the private sector. "Half my work is done in French," he said, "and I'm proof that it's possible — even in predominantly English Ontario. My goal is to see a French business network that will allow Franco-Ontarian businessmen to work in French, to invest together, and to offer each other mutual support."

The use of French in business in Ontario has been greatly facilitated by the fact that French is already employed in federal government offices. In Sudbury, many jobs in the civil service now require a knowledge of French. Secretaries, for example, find it difficult to find positions anywhere if they are not bilingual. The problems experienced by Carolyn Frawley, who has a French mother but never learned the language, show to what extent French has made inroads in the labour force. "Everywhere I go, they ask if I can work in French," said Frawley, who was driving a taxi while looking for an office job. Ironically, if she stays in Sudbury and wants to work as a secretary, she will have to learn French. This realization was prompting her to consider taking a French immersion course in Quebec or in France.

The policies of the Ontario government have also contributed to greater use of French. The rapid growth since 1976 of French services in the provincial courts, for example, has increased the use of French in law firms. Sudbury's Lacroix, Forest, and Delfrate conducts about half its work in French and insists that all new partners be bilingual. Labour specialist Richard Pharand also works increasingly in the language. "English people laugh when they see *cabinet juridique* on my sign outside," he said. "But I have a French as well as an English practice now, so that's the way it's going to be."

The co-operative movement is another way the French community has chosen to enlarge its presence in the economy. In Franco-Ontario, the movement dates back to the 1940s when a network of organizations was developed in banking and agriculture. Today, the *caisses populaires* still play an important role in the lives of Franco-Ontarians. About 200,000 members had over $700 million in savings in seventy-five *caisses* across the province in 1982. The Ontario credit unions have their own federation and are also affiliated with the Desjardins *caisses populaires* movement in Montreal. The Quebec organization insures their loans and savings, administers their employees' pension plan, and gives them access to a central computer for their banking operations.

In the Sudbury area there are fourteen *caisses populaires*, a co-operative funeral home and two food co-ops. The Association canadienne-française de l'Ontario and some professors at Laurentian University have recently been trying to expand the network of co-operatives in the Sudbury area. The initial work was done by Marie-Elisabeth Brunet, who worked with the ACFO from 1972 to 1977. After studying co-operatives in north-western Quebec, she helped set up a food co-operative in the French town of Hanmer, which in turn stimulated a second project in Chelmsford. The expansion of the co-operative movement is now in the hands of Gérard Lafrenière. The former head of continuing education at Laurentian University, he took a year off to study the co-operative movement in Quebec and launched a full study program on co-operatives, in French, in the fall of 1982.

Lafrenière is a bear of a man with a rollicking sense of humour and an eye for the absurd. The son of a farmer, he never expected to go to university. When he graduated from high school, he worked as a lumberjack near Alexandria and as a tobacco picker in southern Ontario. On a whim, he enrolled at the University of Sudbury and went on to become a teacher and professor.

Since high school, Lafrenière has functioned in both French and English worlds quite happily and describes himself as "a cultural hybrid." But he is not willing to surrender the French side of his life, and considers it in danger. "I'm from this part of Canada," he said, "and I intend to stay here. I don't see Quebec as the promised land: French culture must flourish here. However, if we don't develop some kind of economic infrastructure in French, we'll become folklorized and nothing more than a ethnic group."

Lafrenière arrived at this view by watching the progressive anglicization of his son. "We speak French at home and my son goes to French school," he explained. "But he shows no interest at all in French and is being gradually assimilated into the English community. All his friends are English." Lafrenière's teenage daughter does not have the same attitude. She has French friends and shows an attachment to the culture of Nouvel-Ontario.

Lafrenière interprets this difference in attitude between his children this way: His daughter believes that French is important because it is the language of home and family life. His son, on the other hand, looks to the world of work for cues—and finds few of them in French. "When I go to a gas station with him, I speak English to the attendant. When I shop, I speak English to the salesperson. As far as my son is concerned, all the important things in life take place in English."

According to Lafrenière, the co-operative movement is well suited to the mentality of the French because they like working in a collective way. Lafrenière himself is active in a food co-operative in Hanmer. The co-operative has 160 members, most of them mining families, who contribute four hours of work a month to the project. With its religious calendars and pictures of Jesus on the walls, the co-operative is reminiscent of a friendly country store in an old French-Catholic parish. "The working language here is French," noted the full-time manager of the co-operative. "We're unilingual. We take English-speaking members, but they must agree to work in French."

Lafrenière's dream is to establish a network of co-operatives that would permit francophones in the Sudbury area to do a large part of their business in their mother tongue. "There is no reason," he says, "why all kinds of other activities—car repair shops and gas stations, for example—could not run on the same basis as the Hanmer grocery store."

It is difficult for the people of Nouvel-Ontario to carve out a place for themselves in the economy. There are few French businessmen available to do it and the English majority in Ontario is not particularly sympathetic to the idea. Nevertheless, determined individuals like Gaston Demers, Jacques de Courville Nicol, and Gérard Lafrenière are emerging, and circumstances are more favourable now than ever before.

The change that is affecting Franco-Ontario the most is the resumption of what could be called the "Quebec connection." During the sixties and seventies, links with Quebec were not very fruitful for Nouvel-Ontario or French communities elsewhere in

Canada. Quebec was too preoccupied with its own cultural future to show much interest in the francophones beyond its borders. But the inward-looking approach that characterized Quebec during the long period preceding its 1980 referendum on sovereignty-association is being replaced by new concerns, particularly with regard to greater participation in economic life. One-third of Canadian students enrolled in business administration courses are in Quebec. The business pages of Quebec's French newspapers are expanding. Salaries for commentators on the economy are starting to exceed those of political columnists. Quebec companies are branching out across Canada and are already in a position to offer interesting careers to bilingual francophones in other provinces.

Ties between French business people in Ontario and Quebec are multiplying. Gaston Demers and Conrad Lavigne, for example, are on the boards of French firms in Quebec. The Malette brothers of Timmins are developing lumber plants in Trois-Rivières, while the Perron lumber entrepreneurs of La Sarre, Quebec, are active in northern Ontario. These bonds between Quebec and Franco-Ontario are likely to continue growing. It will take time before Canadians realize that Montreal has become the centre of an economy that operates principally in French. Among those to benefit from it will be francophones outside Quebec. For the first time in their history, they may be able to participate in a nation-wide business network that functions in French and is sympathetic to their economic goals.

Part II

The Burden of the Past

Nouvel-Ontario is like the head of Janus: it faces in two directions at one and the same time, looking toward the future as well as back to the past. On the one hand, a confident, young leadership is encouraging a Quiet Revolution in cultural and economic life, while on the other, a more traditional group is still preoccupied with the hardships of the past.

The two faces of Janus co-exist within the minds of everyone in the French community: they alternate between hope and despair over the future of Franco-Ontarian life. Optimism flows from the belief that a culture based on new values can thrive and progress, while despondency comes from the suspicion that only survival is possible—and perhaps not even that.

If the past cannot be filed away in the archives of the community's collective consciousness, it is because so many problems associated with history are still alive. Even the most optimistic are coloured by it. Francophones cannot forget their history, and harbour bitter memories of one event in particular: the adoption in 1912 of Regulation 17, which closed French schools in Ontario. The law was repealed in 1927, but its spirit continues to affect the present educational system.

The past survives in another form as well: in the apprehensive feelings of the English majority regarding the use of French in public life. Many francophones are so intimidated by the English that they willingly confine their language to home, church, and cultural activities. This continuous relegation of French to a strictly private world erodes the vitality of the community and causes deep resentment.

The adoption of French as a second official language in Ontario and the greater availability of provincial government services in French would help dissipate the widespread conviction among Franco-Ontarians that their language is not accepted by the English majority. But the steadfast refusal of the provincial government to do this only intensifies the feeling among the French minority that they should keep their language and culture hidden.

Every segment of the French population is influenced by the burden of the past, restraining even the most optimistic among them. Those who are most weighed down by their history become invisible French. Others, so worn down by the struggle, are tempted by assimilation—a situation that is aggravated by internal disputes in the French community.

Chapter 4

When your child comes home from school and has trouble speaking French, his mother tongue, the time has come to do something about it, at least if you are the kind of parent who has pride in your own language and culture.

Roland Desroches, parent, Penetanguishene

We left a school that had a French atmosphere, that was comfortable, for a real monster, an English school that put up with one class in French a day. I felt like a black in a white school ...
    The École secondaire de la Huronie will never close its doors and will always remain a legend. Its spirit will never disappear.

Basile Dorion, former student, Penetanguishene[1]

The Spirit of Regulation 17

In 1979 the La Corvée theatre troupe of Ottawa presented its first performance of *La parole et la loi*, an angry play about Regulation 17, which banned teaching in French in Ontario public schools from 1912 to 1927. Since then, the company has taken the play to packed houses all over Franco-Ontario. The play's reception is largely due to its theme—*la survivance*—the fight to survive, which has been the principal concern of the Franco-Ontarian community since the late nineteenth century.

When the play started touring, Franco-Ontario was in the midst of its most bitter school crisis in a decade. A battle royal was taking place in the oldest French settlement in Ontario: Penetanguishene, on Georgian Bay. In this historic town, French parents were running a parallel and illegal French high school in an old post office. Since 1977 they had been pleading with the Simcoe County Board of Education for a separate French school. In desperation, they asked the Association canadienne-française de l'Ontario for a director and the Association des enseignants franco-ontariens for teachers. Then, in September 1979, they hoisted the green and white Franco-Ontarian flag[2] and opened l'École de la Huronie. Born out of a resistance movement, the school became a symbol for francophones across the country of the struggle to survive. Every French organization in Ontario—and many across Canada—rallied to support the school.

The struggle for an independent French high school in Penetanguishene started with the victims of poor French education—francophone students in the town's local high school. It all began on November 3, 1976, when a determined grade thirteen student, Denise Jaiko, wrote a long and detailed letter to the Simcoe County board's Comité consultatif de langue française demanding that the École secondaire Penetanguishene Secondary School become bilingual in fact as well as in name.

Until 1966, Penetanguishene had had a small, primarily French high school, which the students liked; but it was closed when the larger and more modern secondary school opened. The new school was supposed to respond to the needs of French students in the area, but its failure to provide an adequate program for them had been an issue for many years. Denise Jaiko brought the matter to a head.

French language and culture had no status in the school, she charged. The majority of the students were of French background, yet the atmosphere was English. Certain courses were supposed to be available in French but even these had become anglicized. Student Victor Dupuis described his geography course this way: "Discussion in the classroom took place in English because the teacher was an English person who had taken a course in French with the idea of teaching us in our own language—with the goal of assimilating us, would be more like it."[3] To rectify the situation, Jaiko demanded that the school make twenty-four changes affecting policy and personnel.

The school, however, refused to make any improvements. A year later, the Comité consultatif de langue française, which is there to advise the school board on French issues, decided that the only solution was to ask for a separate French school. The Simcoe County board, which is controlled by anglophones, turned down the request. Education minister Bette Stephenson and Premier William Davis would not intervene. French students and parents refused to accept the verdict. Instead, they set up École de la Huronie and vowed they would never abandon it until the authorities gave in and granted them a separate French school.

The French community in the area was split over the issue. Many people wanted a separate French school, but others considered that Penetanguishene Secondary School had enough French. Some families felt that a predominantly English education was the only way to guarantee their children equal opportunities in the job market.

The response of the English in Penetanguishene was largely antagonistic. The town council claimed the parallel school contravened zoning regulations and sought, unsuccessfully, to secure a court injunction to close it. As hostility mounted, the resolve of the students toughened, and many became politicized for the first time.

"I really hate politics," said student Marie-Thérèse Maurice. "It's the most crooked business in the world. At first, I didn't even know that Bette Stephenson was the minister of education. Nor did I realize that politics and education went hand in hand. I'm not so dumb now." Micheline Marchand found out that "since Stephenson's policies apply to all of Ontario, we're fighting not only for ourselves, but for all the francophones in the province."[4]

As the crisis deepened, the Penetanguishene students formed a touring information caravan to raise money for École de la Huronie. Speaking in French schools from Ottawa to Hearst, they became heroes for 30,000 French high school students across the province. To further publicize their struggle, students staged demonstrations and sit-ins outside the provincial legislature in Toronto. The press converged on Penetanguishene and the French community received moral support from Prime Minister Pierre Trudeau, Quebec Premier René Lévesque, Commissioner of Official Languages Max Yalden, and Stuart Smith, leader of the Ontario Liberal party. Yet Premier Davis still refused to intervene. It was only on the eve of the Quebec referendum on sovereignty-association—more than three years after Denise Jaiko wrote her original letter—that Davis finally gave in and announced that Penetanguishene could have a separate French high school.

It was an important but ambiguous victory for Franco-Ontarians. Political pressure, not entrenched rights, had given Penetanguishene a French high school. The French knew that the right to separate French shools—and independent French school boards— was what they needed. The French consultative committees attached to Ontario school boards, they discovered, had no power. Roland Desrochers, who headed the Comité consultatif de langue française in Penetanguishene at the time, found dealing with the local board extremely frustrating. "We should have been consulted by the Simcoe County Board of Education, but we weren't until the policies were a *fait accompli*: most of the time our recommendations were ignored and when they were adopted they were put in motion in such a way that they were not acceptable to the students and teachers we represented."[5] Premier Davis, however, has always been opposed to giving Franco-Ontarians their own school boards. The French knew, therefore, that it was just a matter of time before the next Penetanguishene cropped up. Regulation 17—in modern dress—was far from dead.

The play *La parole et la loi* is about the plight of people who have lived through situations like the one in Penetanguishene. In a series of sketches, it describes how Irish Bishop Michael Fallon, Conservative Premier James Whitney, and the Orange Order tried to stamp out French in Ontario during the first quarter of the twentieth century. What makes the play so effective is the way it moves back and forth between past and present.

Half way through the play, "Premier Davis" comes on stage holding a copy of the old Regulation 17. "There are only two classes of Primary Schools in Ontario: Public Schools and Separate Schools," he reads. "In the case of French-speaking pupils, French may be used as the language of instruction and communication; but such use of French shall not be continued *beyond the second grade*."

Turning to the audience, Davis explains: "For a long time francophones have been causing problems in Ontario. I can say that the problem is nearly non-existent ... The repatriation of the constitution will insure that this conflict will not arise again. I shall never consider the French language as an official one," he says resolutely. "The francophones in this province are a minority just like the Ukrainians, the Germans, and the Indians. Therefore, they do not have the right to special demands."[6]

Because of the attitudes of the Ontario government, the memories of Regulation 17 have never been laid to rest. Even without a return to the old law, many Franco-Ontarians feel their community is being constantly whittled away. Schools alone can no longer safeguard their language and culture. Many schools in Franco-Ontario are now completely French: in the Sudbury region, for example, there are forty-one French elementary schools and four large high schools. Yet English is spoken almost as much as French, even in predominantly French neighbourhoods such as Moulin à Fleur. At the end of *La parole et la loi*, the scenes juxtapose the older generation, who contested Regulation 17, with their children and grandchildren, who are being absorbed into the English milieu through entertainment, books, and the media.

"My problem is that books in French cost too much," says one girl in the play. "Yes, well, as far as I'm concerned, all the good music is in English. French music is boring! How can I dance disco to Robert Paquette?"

"My problem is that my boyfriend is English; so I'm becoming assimilated and, I must admit, I like it," says another.

"I started work as a secretary for the government," explains a third. "My boss is English so I had to learn shorthand and typing in English. It's as simple as that."

And finally: "It all started when I was pretty small. I was addicted to Walt Disney films. As I got older, it got worse. Even though I tried not to, I only liked English movies and TV programs. They were always exciting. The people in that world looked as though they were having such a good time that I said to myself: if I were English I would have a much more interesting life."[7]

For many Franco-Ontarians—especially the older people—the historic notion of *la survivance* is still the guiding ideology for the community. *La survivance* meant creating large families who lived off the land and clustered around the local school and church. This formula for cultural survival worked in a traditional society that could remain apart from modern industrial life, but it ceases to have much meaning in an urban environment. It can hardly serve the young people whose modern-day predicaments are described in the final scenes of *La parole et la loi*.

In Quebec, *la survivance* died out as a way of seeing the world only with the death of Premier Maurice Duplessis in 1959 and the start of the Quiet Revolution in 1960. Quebec ceased being a predominantly rural society in the 1920s; nevertheless, political and clerical leaders did not encourage people in the cities to make their mark in business. Instead, they promoted the idea of a segregated society where the English directed the economy and the French controlled political and cultural institutions. In their view, the key to survival still lay with ownership of the land and a closely knit community revolving around the rural parish.

The French in Ontario also clung to the security of *la foi, la langue, la race,* faith, language, and race. But they suffered from a constant handicap compared with the French in Quebec. A strong school and church have been the cornerstones for *la survivance;* but whereas in Quebec these institutions were strong fortresses, beyond the reach of the English, in Ontario, they were constantly under attack.[8]

The English in Quebec never had to fight for their schools.[9] The provincial government was always sensitive to English demands for quality education. Until 1964, in fact, they tolerated a system of school taxes which gave the English Protestant school boards far more revenue than the boards which were Catholic and mainly French. The Franco-Ontarians have not been so fortunate. Until 1969 there were no separate French public high schools. As the Penetanguishene case illustrates, Franco-Ontarians do not have the right to separately run schools, let alone autonomous school boards. In 1982 most of Ontario's 72,000 francophone elementary school students attended separate French schools, but of 28,000 French high-school students, 6,500 attended schools that shared facilities with an English sector. In some cases, only a percentage of their subjects was taught in French. French education in Ontario does not yet rest on a solid foundation. As a result, the community remains obsessed by the school question, and cannot shake itself free of the idea of *la survivance* and of the educational and clerical elite that has always acted as its spokesmen.[10]

Systematic suppression of French—particularly French schools— has been part of Ontario politics for the past century. It is not surprising that the fight for schools is now part of Franco-Ontarian culture. The school issue has a history that predates Confederation, although it was not always so pressing. At one time, French schools—and autonomous French school boards—were part of Ontario's public and separate Catholic school systems.[11] Troubles arose in the 1880s when, all across the country, the English in provinces with sizeable French minorities began to feel threatened by the French living among them.

The problem, as Robert Choquette describes it in *Language and Religion,*[12] revolved around the rise in Canada of nativism: an intense opposition to minorities based on their supposed foreign connections. In the late nineteenth century this nativism was most apparent between Protestants and Catholics.[13] In Ontario it arose because Protestants felt threatened by the influx of French Catholics from Quebec and Irish Catholics from Ireland. The Protestants, led by the Orangemen and the Protestant Protective Association, feared a Catholic takeover of their province and country.

Slowly, Protestant / Catholic antagonism shifted to become an ethnic, linguistic, and cultural conflict between the French and English. This isolated the French from the Irish Catholics and made their struggle much more difficult. "While the struggle remained a Protestant-Catholic one," writes Choquette, "French and English Catholics stuck together in spite of behind-the-scenes wrangling. Once the fight became primarily linguistic and cultural, however, Catholic solidarity gave way to linguistic and cultural alignments, with Catholic brotherhood becoming a secondary factor."[14]

By the 1880s it was clear to francophones across Canada that the English wanted to get rid of their schools and dampen the power of their communities. In Ontario exclusively French schools were concentrated in Prescott and Russell counties in the east. In 1883, writes Choquette, "the erect ears of the sentinels of Protestantism began to twitch over stories coming from the area." The Orangemen applied pressure and, in 1885, the provincial government passed a law requiring the teaching of English in all schools.

During this time, Toronto newspapers reflected the growing English fear of everything French. The *Mail*, for example, wrote that the "Russell and Prescott schools are nurseries not merely of an alien tongue, but of alien customs, of alien sentiments and ... of a wholly alien people."[15] The government's next move was to pass legislation in 1890 making English the only authorized language in schools, except in the case of students who did not understand English. The suppression of French schools was becoming so severe that Franco-Ontarians had little room left to manoeuvre.

In this same period, the governments of Manitoba, the Northwest Territories, and New Brunswick stopped subsidizing Catholic schools, in violation of the spirit of Article 93 of the British North America Act. These developments frightened Franco-Ontarians because opposition to Catholicism was so closely linked to opposition to the French. The Riel Rebellion in the West had unleashed a wave of anti-French feeling. After Louis Riel was hanged in

59

Manitoba in 1885, the English in that province vowed to crush every vestige of French language and culture. In 1890 they dropped French as an official language in the legislature and courts, and severely limited its use in the schools.

Terrified that their schools were in danger, Franco-Ontarians started to organize. After four years of emotional meetings all over the province, a huge congress of angry Franco-Ontarians, drawn from every sector of the community, met in Ottawa in 1910 to discuss the school question. The organizers, largely clergy, were confident that they could pressure the Ontario government into giving them their own schools and teacher training colleges. "We have seized our share of the land," they declared in one of their brochures. "Let us now demand our share of the teaching."[16]

All of French Canada eagerly followed the proceedings of the congress, which was crowned by a rousing speech by Prime Minister Wilfrid Laurier, who urged Ontario to treat the French the way Quebec treated its English. At the end of the congress, the Association canadienne-française d'éducation d'Ontario (ACFEO) was founded to fight for French school rights. It asked the Ontario government to give the French language official status in elementary and secondary schools and in teacher training institutions. A month later, armed with a lengthy petition demanding equality in education, a delegation from the ACFEO met Premier James Whitney to discuss ways to improve the situation.

The Irish Catholic clergy were very much disturbed by the demands that emerged from the Franco-Ontarian congress. They feared that the ultimate goal of the French was to take over the entire Catholic school system. Prior to the congress, English-speaking Catholic bishops in Ontario had been pressing the Whitney government to give the Catholic school boards a greater share of elementary school grants. In response to their request, the government drafted plans to redistribute funds in their favour. After the ACFEO presented its demands, however, the government suddenly changed its mind. On March 10, 1910, Whitney sent a telling letter to Archbishop McNeil of Toronto explaining why:

> I regret very much that considerations beyond its control have prevented the cabinet from giving proper and full consideration to the propositions laid before it by you some time ago. We fully expected to be in a position to do so before now, but the memorandum sub-

mitted to us on behalf of a Congress of French-Canadians held in Ottawa, has so complicated matters that we find it quite out of the question to deal with the subjects thoroughly during the stress of the sessions.[17]

The Irish Catholics in Ontario thought that a separate Catholic school system was the best way to ensure their religious and ethnic survival. Whitney's letter confirmed their deeply held conviction that the Franco-Ontarians were jeopardizing the system. It gave them the opportunity they were looking for to come out against French schools. The man who led the crusade against French education was Michael Fallon, Bishop of London, Ontario. Supported by the Irish Catholic hierarchy, he made a virtual pact with Whitney to eliminate French schools completely.

Once he showed his anti-French colours, Fallon became the arch-enemy of francophones across Canada. Quebec periodicals, for example, wrote about him with contempt and scorn. In an article written in 1910 in La Revue franco-américaine, Michel Renouf described Fallon's war on the Franco-Ontarians this way: "And they all came: English fanatics, Orangemen, the envious from all races and all sectors, Irish Catholics. They united their efforts to support in his holy war the new Mohammed."[18]

But the alliance of Irish Catholics, Orangemen, and Whitney's Conservative government could not be stopped. The axe fell on the French in 1912 when the government passed Regulation 17 banning schooling in French almost entirely. Students who could not speak English could receive French instruction up to grade three, but after that it was prohibited. In public schools, teaching in French was illegal, and those who broke the law were treated as outlaws.

Franco-Ontarians mobilized immediately to lobby against the repressive policies of the Conservative government. In 1913 the French newspaper Le Droit was launched in Ottawa to fight against Regulation 17; its motto was L'avenir est à ceux qui luttent — The future belongs to those who fight. The ACFEO, however, was the key political mouthpiece of the Franco-Ontarian community in its defence of schools and promotion of the ideology of la survivance. (The organization dropped the reference to education in its name in 1968, when it became simply the Association canadienne-française de l'Ontario [ACFO].)

It was not until 1927—after fifteen years of intense lobbying by Franco-Ontarians, patriotic organizations in Quebec, and French members in the House of Commons—that Regulation 17 was finally amended to allow teaching in French once again. However, it was not formally removed from the statutes until 1944.[19]

Most of the Irish, particularly the clergy, never changed their views on French schools. In the end, the French found allies outside their own community in the heart of Anglo-Protestant Ontario. In the 1920s a group of 150 eminent anglophones, almost all of them Protestant, formed the Unity League to fight for the withdrawal of Regulation 17 and equal rights for the French minority in Ontario and other provinces. Working in close cooperation with the ACFEO, the league organized lectures, circulated pamphlets, and wrote letters to the Ontario government demanding justice for Franco-Ontarians.

The Unity League stressed that bilingualism was Canada's mark of distinction as well as its *raison d'être*. In a prophetic view of English-French relations, the organization warned that the country risked eventual disintegration if French Canadians continued to be repressed. It pointed out that the English minority in Quebec, both Protestant and Catholic, received just treatment from that province's government, while the French minority in the rest of Canada suffered from the violation of clauses in the British North America Act that were intended to protect minorities.[20]

In 1924, three years before Regulation 17 was modified, the president of the league, John Godfrey, wrote a letter to Conservative Premier George Howard Ferguson suggesting that there was widespread support for a shift in policy toward the French minority, and that the time had come for action. "It is a great thing to be prime minister of Ontario," he wrote, "but it will be a much greater accomplishment to have made this contribution to National Unity."[21]

The Franco-Ontarians felt that the efforts of the Unity League contributed greatly towards the resolution of the school problem. Bishop Joseph Hallé, who at the time was a lobbyist for French-Canadian interests in Rome, said: "The Protestants of the Unity League are effecting a magnificent work of union through justice. In the years ahead, impartial history will be compelled to say ... that ... the effort for the re-establishment of peace [and] the government's legal amendment will have been done by laymen and by Protestants."[22]

While the main conflict between French and English was taking place in the schools, another struggle was coming to a head in the Catholic hierarchy. The Irish and the French had long been fighting one another for control of the church and its institutions. In the early 1900s the University of Ottawa, founded in 1866 by the Oblate Order of France, was rife with French-English squabbling.[23] At the centre of the push by the Irish clergy to dominate the Catholic church in Canada were Bishop Michael Fallon of London and Bishop David Joseph Scollard of Sault Ste. Marie. They tried to reduce the French role in the church wherever they could. In addition to opposing French schools, they imposed English priests on French towns and discouraged French Canadians from entering the priesthood. Scollard in particular applied these tactics ruthlessly in French parishes in Nouvel-Ontario, including Capreol, Espanola, Thessalon, and Coniston where the majority of the Catholics were French.[24]

After 1920 relations between the French and Irish worsened. Finally, in 1926, Senator Napoléon Antoine Belcourt, president of the ACFEO, sent a long memorandum to the Vatican on the problems of the French in Ontario and criticized the appointment by Rome of clergy foreign to the mentality and aspirations of French Canadians outside Quebec. He pointed out that Irish clergymen dominated parishes with French majorities. Sixteen noted French Canadians followed suit with a letter to the Pope underlining the need for recognition of French-Canadian rights within the church. Among the petitioners were Ernest Lapointe, the federal minister of justice; Lomer Gouin, a former Quebec premier; and Supreme Court Justices Thibeaudeau Rinfret, P. B. Migneault, and Charles Marcil.

After Regulation 17 was changed in 1927, the church softened its policies towards Franco-Ontarians; nevertheless, dioceses with French minorities continued to try to place English priests in French parishes. Bishop Dignan replaced Scollard as bishop of the Sault Ste. Marie diocese, which covered Nouvel-Ontario, but he was as anti-French as his predecessor. During the 1950s, for example, he tried to stop formation of three French parishes in Sudbury on the grounds that there were no French priests to serve them. He was foiled by a priest at St. Anne's church who recruited Jesuits from Quebec to serve the community.

Although Regulation 17 was finally repealed, the fight for French schools in Ontario has never stopped. Until 1969 French schooling was confined, with certain exceptions, to the elementary level. The French community established private schools at the secondary level, such as Collège du Sacré-Coeur and Collège Notre-Dame in Sudbury, but the ACFEO continued to demand a completely independent French school system supported by the provincial government.

Following the Quiet Revolution in Quebec and the findings of the Royal Commission on Bilingualism and Biculturalism, the Ontario government became more sensitive to the demands of its francophone minority for separate French secondary schools and made various concessions. In 1965, for example, the minister of education allowed Latin, history, and geography to be taught in French, at the discretion of local school boards.[25] Finally, the Ontario government set up a task force, known as the Bériault Committee, to study the question of French secondary schools in the public system. As a result of its recommendations,[26] Bills 140 and 141 were passed in 1968 opening the way for complete French programs in bilingual or separate French secondary schools.

The school question, however, did not die with Bills 140 and 141. While French classes are guaranteed where numbers warrant, separate French schools depend upon the approval of local school boards, most of which are controlled by English-speaking commissioners. To reinforce their language and culture many Franco-Ontarians feel they need separate schools, because where they share schools with the English, French children usually speak English—and the school milieu loses its French character.

In many parts of Ontario, the English show no sympathy for this problem. Since 1969 school conflicts over the issue have erupted throughout the province. The most celebrated case in recent years was in Penetanguishene, but there were earlier battles in Sturgeon Falls, Cornwall, Windsor, and Elliot Lake. These earlier cases were only resolved after the government appointed a mediator or passed special legislation. New Brunswick solved the school question by creating separate French and English boards and a ministry of education composed of French and English divisions, each with its own deputy minister.[27]

In the spring of 1982 the Joint Committee on the Governance of French Language Elementary and Secondary Schools, composed of high-ranking officials in the Ontario government, presented a report to Premier William Davis recommending that French education be available as a basic right and not just "where numbers warrant." It also asked that school boards with 500 French pupils or a 10 per cent French enrolment give jurisdiction over French education to a panel of French trustees. If accepted, these recommendations would meet some of the French community's demands for changes in the status of French education in Ontario.

The reluctance of Ontario to grant autonomy in education means that Franco-Ontarians remain prisoners of the school question and cannot psychologically move on to other issues. Some people suspect the government wants to keep the French community in a state of obsession about schools. Freed from the yoke of fighting for secondary schools and autonomous boards, people might push more forcefully for a separate French university, more government services in French, and official status for French in the legislature and courts.

The problem with *la survivance* as an ideology is that it sees French-Canadian society in very restricted terms. French life is equated with school, church, and cultural activities, and not at all with business, technology, and public life. Many francophones in Sudbury believe that English and French domains should remain separate. Quebec functioned this way until the Quiet Revolution, but now it uses French in all sectors of life, and the goal of the government is to create a "complete society" where the French language prevails everywhere.

Sudbury's traditional elite, which consists primarily of educators and priests, operates with an outdated vision of society that does not correspond with the way most francophones in the city now live. A large percentage of the workers in northern Ontario are miners, skilled workers, and labourers.[28] The children of these people go to high school and expect to have careers in business, science, and technology. French must have a role outside home, church, and cultural associations if it is to continue to be relevant to modern life.

The Catholic elementary schools, the French section of Laurentian University, and the weekly French newspaper Le Voyageur, are examples of important institutions in Sudbury that cannot seem to let go of the old order. Intellectuals and professionals are critical of these organizations, but they fear that if these institutions relinquish their link with the church, they will cease to be French. It is as if the combination of faith, language, and ethnicity is the only way to ensure the survival of the Franco-Ontarian community.

The values represented by the Collège du Sacré-Coeur, founded by the Jesuits in 1913, are still important for the old elite. Originally a classical college that produced well-educated graduates who spoke impeccable French, it changed its name to the University of Sudbury in 1957. In 1960 it became part of the new Laurentian University which amalgamated three religious colleges.

Many Franco-Ontarians with important positions in the community received their basic education at Collège du Sacré-Coeur. The college was, for many of them, a kind of Shangri-La of intellectual and artistic life. Jean Ethier-Blais, literary columnist for Le Devoir in Montreal and a professor of French literature at McGill University, spent his formative years at the college. The Jesuits who taught there, he said, contributed more to his intellectual growth than professors he met later at celebrated universities in France and Germany. Reminiscing about Sacré-Coeur, he became reverent and dreamy-eyed. Sacré-Coeur belongs to an era of Franco-Ontarian life that cannot be recreated, but the remnants of the world it represented live on in Sudbury's Catholic schools and university.

In Sudbury the separate Catholic school board provides the only French elementary school education in Nouvel-Ontario. The Catholic school system has French and English sectors, but the French, who are more numerous, dominate it: the president of the board, for example, is French. French primary schools in the public sector do not exist, because parents feel French cultural values are more protected under a Catholic system. Unlike Catholic schools in Quebec, religious and traditional family values are central to Franco-Ontario's Catholic school program.

Teachers, for example, cannot be divorced or separated and must prove they are practising Catholics. Parents must go to church and baptize their children. This creates problems for everyone, yet people are prepared to go through the motions of

Catholicism—even when they are non-believers—because they are convinced the system is preserving Franco-Ontarian culture. "I'm not a practising Catholic, and I don't really like the policies of the Catholic system," said one parent, "but I feel more protected as a French-speaking person within the Catholic schools."

Some remarkable French professors, many of them Jesuits, teach at Laurentian University. However, the university's French component reflects the past rather than the future. The attachment to old cultural values is evident in the office of André Girouard, the coordinator of the French program. A collection of old black and white photographs of by-gone days in the old French-Canadian parish adorns one wall. Hanging in their midst is a telling quote from the French-Canadian historian François-Xavier Garneau:

> Faithful to the religion of his forefathers, loyal to the laws that were handed down to him, cherishing the language that soothed his ears in the cradle, no one of French-Canadian parentage in Lower Canada has yet denied the three great symbols of his nationality: his language, his laws, his religion.

The program of study available in French at Laurentian University reflects a society that still defines itself in terms of language, philosophy, and the classics. Courses are confined to education, humanities, social sciences, theology, and translation. A new program for students interested in the co-operative movement opened in the fall of 1982, but students interested in business, science, or engineering must take their degrees in English. When the university was created in 1960, about half its students were French. By 1982 they represented only a fifth of the student body and the institution was losing its attraction as a centre of French culture.

The only French newspaper in Sudbury, Le Voyageur, also bears the stamp of the old order. Started in 1968 to replace a weekly diocesan paper, it was funded initially by the French parishes in Sudbury and the Sisters of Charity religious order. Hector Bertrand, a Jesuit, has been editor of Le Voyageur since 1975, when he retired as rector of the University of Sudbury. The editorial policy of the paper has always been clear: the promotion of Catholicism and the rights of Franco-Ontarians.

The main political pressure group of the community, l'Association canadienne-française de l'Ontario, also shows attachment to the ideas surrounding *la survivance*. In recent years, the association has gone beyond the concern for schools which characterized its predecessor, l'Association canadienne-française d'education d'Ontario. The younger group's *service d'animation*, for example, was responsible for promoting the co-operative movement in Sudbury and encouraging the use of French in business. The ACFO also persuaded the city of Sudbury to become officially bilingual and pushed Radio-Canada to open a French radio station. Nevertheless, across the province the organization retains a Catholic perspective characteristic of more traditional times. Its congresses, for example, often open with a mass. Such a thing would be unthinkable for a Quebec organization such as the Société Saint-Jean-Baptiste, which is also concerned with education and language issues. Generally speaking, the Franco-Ontarian community channels its grievances through the ACFO rather than through French members of Parliament or political parties—a legacy of the old feeling that survival depends upon living in a world apart, and that the state is not relevant to the community.

Because Franco-Ontario still defines itself in terms of language and religion, the church—and a number of social and cultural associations—are the most vigorous institutions in the community. Saint-Jean-de-Brébeuf church in Moulin à Fleur, for example, is one of the most important gathering points for the French in Sudbury. The church's priest, André Morin, is very aware of the pivotal role the church plays in the community. People, he said, would go to great lengths to ensure that the church remained strong. In 1980 fire destroyed most of Saint-Jean-de-Brébeuf. To rebuild the church, the 1,200 families of the parish raised one million dollars. Part of the fund-raising campaign was a day-long television show, a telethon, prepared by the community's musicians, artists, and actors.

Even in this exclusively French niche in the community, the long arm of the English occasionally is present. When the final repairs were made to Saint-Jean-de-Brébeuf and a *sortie* sign was placed over the exit, the construction department of the Sudbury regional government announced it would fine the church $200 a day if it did not put up an English sign as well. Father Morin put up the English sign, arranged for an inspection, and then removed it. "This is a French church," he said. "There's no need for English here."

The Centre des jeunes, started in 1950 by the late Albert Régimbal, a Jesuit, is the key cultural organization of the French in Sudbury. Although religion is not forced upon young people who come to the centre for crafts, courses, and community programs, the centre has a Catholic orientation. Monique Cousineau, a dynamic ex-nun, who ran the centre until 1982, has devoted her life to protecting and promoting French in Nouvel-Ontario. Under her direction, the centre became involved in practically every important political issue in the French community. Cousineau herself organized the action groups that pressed for a Radio-Canada radio station and a television production centre.

The Centre des jeunes started off in the basement of St. Anne's church. In September 1981 it moved with great fanfare to a newly renovated former French hospital called Place-Saint-Joseph. Situated close to other important French institutions such as St. Anne's and the Catholic school board offices, Place-Saint-Joseph is the cultural hub of the community. The Centre des jeunes shares the building with eight other organizations, including the Galerie du Nouvel-Ontario, the ACFO, and Prise de Parole.

Cultural groups are central to any minority, but in Sudbury they tend to perpetuate a conception of the community more oriented towards the past than the future. Franco-Ontarians retreat to the church, the Centre des jeunes, and the Catholic school board, for example, because they know they will be able to speak French there in peace. The legacy of Regulation 17 is deeply engrained in the consciousness of the Franco-Ontarians. *La survivance* is the only way they know, so they cling to the organizations that have always protected the community.

Chapter 5

The government cannot allow itself to grant linguistic rights to the Franco-Ontarian minority. Law and tradition forbid it. Its survival and the survival of any other government, no matter what its political orientation, depend upon it. This is why any government that tries to render justice in this domain must do it in a manner that is not apparent. Justice must not appear to be done.

Robert Paris, president,
L'association des juristes d'expression française de l'Ontario[1]

French as a Closet Language

In 1981, amid spirited debate over the constitution, the following advertisement appeared in the national edition of the *Globe and Mail*:[2]

Could this be a future ad:
HELP WANTED   —   GOOD JOBS
In business, government, universities, schools, institutions
(ONLY BILINGUAL CANADIANS NEED APPLY)
(NO HALF-CANADIANS (i.e. unilinguals) WANTED)

Are you a SECOND-CLASS CITIZEN (a unilingual) unable to apply for good jobs when the bilingual constitution takes effect? ...

Don't worry—it will all be done gradually but firmly. You won't even notice that an elite group of bilinguals has been created that runs everything, and that you and everyone else who are merely HALF CANADIANS, are out in the cold ...

Even now, under our present bilingual laws, many National organizations in Toronto print their invoices, receipts, and public documents in both English and French. Even the Ontario government is involved in this. Look at your driver's licence and Chargex invoice ...

It is now time for a serious Canada-wide debate on Bilingualism and Biculturalism before it destroys our country ...

Sponsored by a man from Unionville, Ontario, "in the interests of a greater and United Canada," this advertisement was one of a series that took up prime space in the paper and challenged the idea of bilingualism and a country based upon two founding peoples. Such advertisements, which describe French as a national threat, and books such as *Bilingual Today, French Tomorrow* by Jock V. Andrew, find avid readers across Canada. Many anglophones in Ontario see French as a galloping disease which could, like the contents of Pandora's box, invade society and take over: that is why so many want to put bilingualism under lock and key.

In Quebec and Ontario, bilingual organizations are feared, though for different reasons. Quebec regards official bilingualism, whether in government, business, or school, as a fatal first step towards anglicization and eventual assimilation. In the experience of francophones, when an institution becomes bilingual, English tends to drown out French. In Ontario, English resistance to bilingualism revolves around two questions: power sharing and access to jobs. The establishment of parallel French and English divisions in certain parts of the public administration—say, in education— would necessitate a sharing of responsibilities. But this is something that the English majority is loath to accept. In its opinion, the organization of separate French divisions could lead to the rise of a state within the state.

The English are also wary of policies that grant francophones access to information and programs in their own language, because competence in French then becomes a prerequisite for certain jobs in the civil service. With the expansion of French-immersion programs in schools, many young Ontarians are now bilingual; but since most of their parents are still unilingual, jobs that require facility in the two languages tend to go first to francophones because they are bilingual. About 17,000 anglophone students in Ontario were enrolled in French immersion programs in 1982. According to a study the same year by the Ontario Institute for Studies in Education, the growing presence of young anglophones who speak French is causing apprehension in Ontario. The English majority fears that the burgeoning bilingual generation will become the core of a new Canadian elite that will dominate the country.

The fear of French seems to have deep psychological roots. Anxiety about French is so common among anglophones that some will react in surprising ways when they encounter the language. Furious outbursts—irrational behaviour usually associated with emotional problems—often occur when unilingual anglophones are exposed to French in a store, or even at a party. The feeling that French is threatening may help explain Premier William Davis's inflexible attitudes on the French schools question and Section 133 of the British North America Act, which outlines requirements for official bilingualism.

The resentment of French by the English majority has taken a psychological toll on many Franco-Ontarians. Because they have had painful and disagreeable experiences while speaking their mother tongue, many repress their French selves except when at home or at cultural activities. Many tuck French away in the closet when they go out in public. Some recent incidents from the lives of French people in Sudbury show how this affects day-to-day life:

• Just before Christmas a miner and his wife were walking along Notre-Dame Street in Moulin à Fleur, discussing in French what they would buy their children. "*Une bicyclette pour Marie, peut-être ... des patins pour Jean-Charles?*" I was walking a few paces behind as they continued talking animatedly in French for about fifteen minutes. As they approached the City Centre shopping complex in downtown Sudbury, the crowds became thicker and a silence seemed to descend upon the couple. When the man opened the door of the mall, the conversation finally started up again—in heavily accented English! When the couple left their French neighbourhood of Moulin à Fleur, they shed their language as well.

• During a reception given by the Sudbury Board of Education, English and French board members and their spouses were having a drink before dinner. In a corner, two Franco-Ontarian men were absorbed in a serious conversation in their mother tongue when an anglophone woman suddenly sat down next to them. "You know, I'd appreciate it if you wouldn't speak French," she said, looking at them self-righteously, as if they were in a no-smoking area puffing on strong cigars. The men were taken aback but said nothing in response. Instead, they quietly moved away.

• I was waiting to catch the airport mini-bus at the Holiday Inn in Sudbury with about ten people bound for Toronto and Ottawa. A middle-aged woman and her elderly mother sat by themselves in a corner in the hotel lobby, talking to each other in French. The bus arrived and the woman and her mother ended up sharing a seat with a boy carrying a guitar and a knapsack. For the next half hour, all the way to the airport, the two women conversed only in English. Alone again at the airport, they switched back to French.

Such experiences suggest that many Franco-Ontarians feel confused and ambivalent about their language. Yet they do not lack official encouragement to affirm themselves in public: federal policies on bilingualism, the stance of the Fédération des francophones hors Québec, and the behaviour of their Quebec confrères all offer precedents. Francophones know instinctively that if French is to survive in an urban setting it must have an official place in day-to-day living. But the promotion of French arouses such opposition and resentment from the English majority that many francophones cannot free themselves of the notion that French should be kept under wraps. As a result, Franco-Ontarians tend to look upon French as the language of the home, the church, and cultural activities, and English as the language of business and public life.

In Sudbury, the struggle to gain recognition for French in public has focused upon the federal government because Ottawa appears more favourable to bilingualism than the provincial or municipal authorities. Through the Official Languages Act of 1969 and the Charter of Rights contained in the Canadian constitution, the federal government guarantees French services to minority communities across the country. In principle, francophones in Sudbury can communicate in their mother tongue when they go to the post office, the unemployment insurance office, or the manpower office. Corporations such as Air Canada, which fall under federal jurisdiction, are also required to offer French services. In practice, however, such services are far from adequate.

When I asked French people in Sudbury whether the federal government provided French services, many would answer: "Well ... yes ... more or less." Then there would be a long pause while they decided whether or not to go into details. I spoke to most people in French, but my accent immediately identified me as English. The question people seemed to be asking themselves when they first met me was: Would this English person listen calmly to criticism of French services, or would she fly into a rage? Interestingly, people tended to respond according to what language we spoke. If we were conversing in English, they were reluctant to criticize; if in French, they would pour out their bitterness and frustration. Although I was still identified as an anglophone, the fact that I spoke French made me appear sympathetic and thus trustworthy. Once this had been established, every francophone had his or her own personal story of shabby treatment by a federal government department.

Radio-Canada reporter Marie-Elisabeth Brunet, who worked as a community organizer for the Association canadienne-française de l'Ontario, learned more about the problem than the average person. Talking about her experiences with the post office and the manpower office, she displayed a weariness with the attitudes of federal government officials. "It took me three years," she said, "just to get the post office to put out French tax forms as a matter of routine. The first year I asked for a form they complained they couldn't find them. The next year they put some out in a corner where they were hardly visible. It was only the following year that they set up a kiosque with publicity and tax forms in the two languages." The manpower office was no better. Working with her local member of Parliament, she finally obtained French manpower training programs in the Sudbury region, but the effort was undermined by manpower counsellors who neglected to tell francophones that such courses were available.

Anita Brunet-Lamarche of Prise de Parole publishing house also had problems with the manpower office. "When I got married I decided to change my name on my social security card, so I went to manpower to do it. When I spoke to the clerk in French, she said: 'Do you speak English?'" Brunet-Lamarche said she did, but asked to be served in French. At that point the clerk marched into another area of the office and cried out for all to hear: "There's a girl out here who refuses to speak English. Can someone come out to serve her!"

"You have to be willing to fight for French services," she explained with resignation in her voice. "They're there, but not automatic." Brunet-Lamarche is from the small town of Alban, and has lived in Sudbury since 1967. All her life she has been conscious of her lack of rights as a francophone. When she was a child her father changed his name because he couldn't get a job as a French Canadian in Windsor. Although her generation has seen some improvements, Brunet-Lamarche has experienced her share of humiliations. One of her first jobs in Sudbury was in a jewellery store where the owner forbade the employees to speak French among themselves. Later she worked as a receptionist for an optician: she would answer the phone and announce the name of shop followed by *bonjour*. After the Parti Québécois came to power in 1976, some callers objected to *bonjour* and told her that if she wanted to speak French she could "go to Quebec." Now she works entirely in French with Prise de Parole and uses French in most of her personal and social life. She believes in the right of francophones to services in their own language and is willing to fight for them, but she admits that to insist on French in public requires a thick skin.

The Canadian Broadcasting Corporation provides another example of the federal government's failure to give the French community a place of its own in its network of services. Although Sudbury is more than one-third French, it was not until 1978 that francophones acquired their own production unit for radio, after six years of lobbying by a committee headed by Monique Cousineau of the Centre des jeunes. Unfortunately, the station does not address itself to a broad section of the population. Like Radio-Canada in Montreal, it serves only a restricted cultural elite. This is acceptable in Montreal, where there is a wide choice of radio stations. But in Sudbury, the high-brow programming of Radio-Canada discriminates against the blue-collar workers who form the majority of the French population. The private French radio station in Sudbury, CFBR, is simple and unpretentious. Radio-Canada, on the other hand, intimidates a large portion of the population. "People are reluctant to participate in phone-in shows," said one Radio-Canada reporter. "When you ask them why, they say their French isn't good enough."

The constant pressure of the community for better government services is starting to pay off. In May 1981 Monique Cousineau presented a brief to the Canadian Radio and Television Commission on behalf of Franco-Ontarians, asking for a French television production unit. Installation of such a division is now a top priority for Radio-Canada. In November 1981, in response to a steady stream of complaints about federal services, the Commissioner of Official Languages opened an office in Sudbury. Headed by a militant Acadian, Jeanne Renault, it is forcing local federal offices to improve their services in French.

According to the office of official languages, French services are poor. But this is not because there is a lack of trained French-speaking personnel working in employment centres, unemployment insurance offices, and post offices. To the amazement of the office, most francophones who have risen up the federal hierarchy show no desire to work in, or identify themselves as, French. Many have anglicized their names—Pierre has become Pete, Gérard is now Jerry—so that they are indistinguishable from their anglophone colleagues. They are reluctant to promote French services or a bilingual image in the federal government because they are afraid of ruffling the feathers of the English. Career advancement, they believe, depends upon their keeping a low profile on issues concerning the use of French.

With the exception of Air Canada, which was still unashamedly unilingual in Sudbury in 1982 and the object of a clean-up campaign by the office of official languages, most federal departments and agencies in the city are equipped to offer full French services. But they present an English facade to the public that discourages francophones from speaking their mother tongue. As a result, some senior federal officials are under the impression that there is little demand from the public for French services. "It's only natural that they think that," said Jeanne Renault. "When a francophone comes into an unemployment insurance office, worried that he might not get his cheque, the last thing he wants to do is risk getting someone mad by asking to speak to a French-speaking officer. If the office had a bilingual image, if the receptionist spoke French as well as English, francophones would speak French. Most figure services are only available in English."

The more localized the level of government, the more resistance there is to bilingual services. While federal services in French are far from sufficient, at least they exist. At the municipal level, however, such services are no more than token. Sudbury proclaimed itself officially bilingual in 1972, after which traffic directions and municipal signs became bilingual. Some municipal literature is also available in the two languages and an on-the-spot translator is offered to anyone who wants information in French from the departments at city hall.

French and English, however, do not have anything approaching equal status. Bilingual services, for example, are not available as a matter of course from the staff of various city departments. This would mean making bilingualism a requirement for certain jobs. Although 40 per cent of the Sudbury region is French, the unions are against bilingualism at the municipal level, and so is the English population. Recreational and other programs offered by the city tend to be unilingual. "Pamphlets are bilingual," explained a Macdonald-Cartier student, "but the programs are not. I wanted to take tennis lessons last summer, but they were not available in French." According to Sudbury francophones, city officials always require more justification for French services than for English ones. After the city became officially bilingual, francophone parents pressured the city to match its English day-care program with a similar one in French. They finally obtained the service, but only after a long and frustrating battle.

The status of French in Sudbury is also reflected in the workings of the city council. In 1982 the mayor of Sudbury, Maurice Lamoureux, was bilingual, while the regional chairman, Tom Davies, was unilingual. Although a third of the councillors were francophones, meetings were held exclusively in English, and agendas and minutes were printed in English only. Certain by-laws, however, were published in both languages. Even in the small surrounding municipalities, which are more French than Sudbury, English is the language of the town council. Rayside-Balfour usually has a French mayor; nevertheless, meetings are held in English because there is always at least one unilingual English councillor—and his language takes precedence.

Along with a number of other municipalities with large French minorities, Sudbury receives grants from the Ontario government to promote the use of French. This program is not aimed at making municipal government bilingual; instead it provides French languages training for anglophone employees. A government's commitment to bilingualism can usually be gauged by the bureaucracy set up to implement it. In Sudbury in 1982, this consisted of one junior-level person whose main duties were to translate documents and act as an interpreter.

In Ontario the real obstacle to widespread use of French in the public domain is the provincial government, which does not want to become subject to Section 133 of the British North America Act. Under this section, legislation, agenda, minutes, and of course, court services, must be available in both languages.

Strange as it may seem, conversion to official bilingualism would not result in major bureaucratic changes within the Ontario government. It would be necessary to translate the statutes and publish future legislation in the two languages. But half of the requirement of Section 133—court services in French—is already in the process of being met. Since 1975 Ontario's Attorney-General, Roy McMurtry, has gradually and discreetly built up a network of bilingual court services across the province. A case like that of Gérard Filion, the former president of Marine Industries who was refused a French trial in Toronto in 1978, is not likely to recur.

Criminal trials in French are now available to every Franco-Ontarian, while French services in civil, family, and small claims courts are accessible to more than 80 per cent of the population. The main gap in the system is the Supreme Court of Ontario, which offers French services only in the Ottawa, Toronto, and Prescott-Russell areas. To support the program, the Ontario government has translated many of the statutes and published a special English / French dictionary of legal terms. Lawyers in Ontario who want to practise in both languages can take their law degrees in French and English at the University of Ottawa, which receives government subsidies for the program. According to Robert Paris, president of the Association des juristes d'expression française de l'Ontario, more and more anglophone lawyers in Ontario are learning to practise in French. "A quarter of the members of our association are English-speaking—a very encouraging sign."

Acceptance of Section 133 would have tremendous symbolic significance for Franco-Ontarians because it would establish that they have a right to exist as a defined linguistic group. But the Ontario government has never wanted its francophone community to enjoy this right. Consequently, Franco-Ontarians feel that the services they receive in the courts and elsewhere are privileges that may not be permanent. Despite the stance of Premier Davis, French civil servants who work for the Ontario government believe that eventually the province will become officially bilingual. "Many English-speaking people are still very unsympathetic to the idea," commented one senior bureaucrat, "but attitudes are changing. Anglophones have mixed feelings about French. They want their children to speak the language, but they're against official bilingualism. But I believe that this approach will change with the younger generation."

Franco-Ontarians, however, still have the impression that their language falls into the category of public nuisance. Many are reluctant to ask for services in French. The insecurity of francophones is reflected most poignantly when they appear in court. Sudbury lawyer Richard Pharand has been following the course of French trials since they began. He said that francophones who are charged with an offence hesitate to ask for a trial in French even though they have a right to it. "They already feel vulnerable because they've been charged with something. They think they're demanding a favour when they ask for a trial in French, so although many cannot speak adequate English, they accept a trial in English just the same."

The growth and centralization of the provincial bureaucracy in Toronto since 1960 has had disastrous effects upon the availability and quality of French services in every sphere. In the past, the French community provided health, social, and educational services to its own people through institutions administered by religious orders. When the government took over, the French component in these institutions began to fade.[3]

In the 1960s important community institutions in Franco-Ontario folded or blended into predominantly English organizations and lost their French character. Collège du Sacré-Coeur, for example, was once an autonomous French institution with a renowned tradition. All that remains of it is the bilingual University of Sudbury, buried in the largely English campus of Laurentian University. Laurentian Hospital once functioned almost entirely in French. Though the board remains mainly francophone, some French services are disappearing.

The Ontario government has a minister to co-ordinate French language services, and full-time co-ordinators in departments such as health, and social and community services. Certain government agencies like the Ontario Arts Council and the educational television network have French sectors. But the government has a long way to go before it can claim to have a satisfactory network of French services.

This is why the French minority in Ontario and other provinces has been demanding that separate and parallel social, community, and educational institutions be developed and placed under its direct control. The Association canadienne-française de l'Ontario and the Fédération des francophones hors Québec pressed for this throughout the 1981 federal-provincial talks on the constitution. According to these organizations, the articles on minority language rights in education contained in the Charter of Rights in the constitution give the French nothing more than they have now. In their opinion, the French communities must obtain the *right* to run their own school boards, not just the privilege of having French schools.

Historian Pierre Savard, who teaches at the University of Ottawa, describes the resistance in Ontario to bilingualism and the resulting withdrawal of the Franco-Ontarians: "We are living in a world in which the two linguistic groups are becoming polarized, more so than before, each one tenaciously clinging to its respective identity. In this conflict between these powerful realities, the Franco-Ontarians will continue to live their peaceful life. Some of them will retreat further into the oblivion of their marginality and others will actually become invisible, hiding their embarrassing origins. Only a small number will eventually take advantage of their situation as intermediaries between the two large linguistic groups."[4]

In Ontario many refuse to muffle their French identities but are exhausted by the fight for a place in public life. Some dream of the cultural peace they could enjoy by moving to Quebec. One of them is Radio-Canada journalist Marie-Elisabeth Brunet. Although not from Quebec, Brunet predicts she will one day end up living there, even though she realizes Quebecers often look down on Franco-Ontarians. "I'm a third generation Franco-Ontarian, but I don't know whether I have the heart to stay in Ontario and bring up children here," she said. "It's a constant fight to live in French in Ontario."

Chapter 6

i am the perfect
canadian.
i am the franco-ontarian
in the burned-out woolworth
of his dreams.

. . . .

memories of timmins
ontario stick to my
body like
frost.
aunts and uncles
dance in my head
like the night before
christmas.
i live in toronto ontario.
i have a pocket larousse

with 32,000 words.
i trip over my own
tongue.
my tongue detaches itself
from my mouth and
struggles down yonge st
like a hurt dog.
vive le québec libre.

vive le québec libre.
i am the perfect
canadian.
i am the franco-ontarian
looking for the fire escape
in the demolished
  woolworth
of his dreams.

Patrice Desbiens, "la chérie canadienne," 1979[1]

Assimilation—
A Cultural Choice?

Francophones in Sudbury who are determined to preserve their culture always find it discouraging to visit École secondaire Macdonald-Cartier, one of four French high schools in the Sudbury region. The school is run entirely in French, but the babble of talk in the corridors, cafeteria, and school yard contains a surprising amount of English. Many conversations take place in two languages, starting in one and finishing in the other. Schools like Macdonald-Cartier show the influence of the surrounding English environment. Among the students, the first signs of assimilation are already apparent.

Most of the students at Macdonald-Cartier have been in French schools since grade one, but they have picked up an excellent command of English from a variety of sources—television and radio, an English neighbourhood, or a parent who does not speak French. English comes as easily as French to most young Franco-Ontarians—in some cases more easily: consequently, they move like quick silver from one language to the other, depending upon the topic and the context.

Unlike the French or English in Quebec, young Franco-Ontarians don't seem to mind which language they speak. They are equally at home in both, and the tangled politics of language does not determine their behaviour. The one place where French usually prevails is in the home. Some families feel so strongly about their cultural origins that they have a French-only rule as soon as members step in the door. In these homes, children learn that French is sacred to family life and that English is not welcome. Outside the home, students must also speak French in the classroom, at church, and in cultural organizations such as the Centre des jeunes.

But in the corridors of Macdonald-Cartier and on the streets, English often takes precedence. This happens usually because French culture encompasses such a limited range of interests.[2] Nobody in Sudbury can live a satisfactory life completely in French. Films, magazines, records, television, advertising—all the manifestations of the consumer society—are in English. Jobs in management, science, and technology are also in English. Although this is starting to change, most occupations associated with French minority life are still restricted to teaching, the church, and certain professions such as law and accounting. Because of this, the francophone minority—especially the youth—look to the culture of the English majority for many of their activities.[3] They speak English not necessarily because they feel it is superior to French, but because their lives are compartmentalized: French prevails in certain domains and English in others. When they discuss matters associated with their English world, they find it perfectly normal to speak English rather than French.

The students at Macdonald-Cartier express differing views about their French heritage. Some show great loyalty to their French origins, while others consider themselves to be already English. Many call themselves bilingual Canadians and see no advantage to living exclusively in French. Biculturalism is the only way of life they can imagine, and their hopes for the future reflect this.

Viviane, the daughter of a miner from the town of St. Charles, wants to study advertising and publicity at the University of Toronto. She hopes eventually to work in Sudbury in English and French. "I want to marry a French person like myself and run a completely French home," she said. "That's very important to me. But I like being part of two cultures. I would never want to live in Quebec. There are too many problems there between French and English."

Diane, whose father runs an insurance business with a predominantly French clientele, is registering for a fashion merchandising course in Florida. When she graduates, she also wants to work in Sudbury. Diane knows she may have to work mainly in English, but she expects to have an active personal and social life in French. "I'm a bilingual Canadian with a French heritage," she said. "I will stay French, but I like the English part of my life. I would find it difficult to live in Quebec because there are too many tensions. I like living in both cultures."

Jean, president of the students council at Macdonald-Cartier, wants his life to be more French than Viviane's or Diane's. He hopes to achieve this by becoming a teacher and working in a French school in Sudbury. "I don't feel that my culture is threatened. I intend to marry a French girl and work in French."

Not all students at Macdonald-Cartier like living in two cultures. Bernard, for example, is planning to enrol in Montreal's École des hautes études commerciales and settle in Quebec for good. Both his parents come from the town of Noëlville; his father is a superintendent in the Catholic school board of Sudbury. His brother has already moved to Montreal where he works for a large national corporation.

"My brother used to work in Thunder Bay," he said. "When a promotion came up, his company gave him the option of moving to Montreal or Toronto. He chose Montreal and is very happy there. I'm going to Quebec because I want to live in a place where people aren't afraid of speaking French. I'm tired of being ridden by the English. We speak English even when we are among ourselves. Look around you in this cafeteria. You see it right here, and in a completely French school!" he shouted with disgust. "I want to live somewhere where it's normal to speak French. In Sudbury we are not encouraged to speak our language."

Other students, who do not care whether they continue to live in French or not, are slowly being absorbed by English society. Sandra predicts that she will be speaking very little French ten years from now. She is losing her French culture because she speaks English at home and finds few opportunities to speak French outside of the classroom. "My mother is French, but my father is English," she explained. "He can't speak French, so we speak English at home. The only place where I speak French is at school, and I don't think I'm very good at it." Sandra calls herself a bilingual Canadian and insists that she is bicultural, but she is so insecure about her ability to speak French that she will not risk enrolling in a French university program. She intends to take a social work degree in English and predicts she will marry an anglophone and move to Toronto.

It is too early to say what will happen to these young Franco-Ontarians as they move into adulthood. Sociologist Calvin Veltman, who has done extensive research on minorities in Canada and the United States, sees four crucial stages for minorities who want to preserve their culture: the young Franco-Ontarians at Macdonald-Cartier have clearly passed through two already. When children are very young, their language is determined largely by their parents' behaviour. When they begin school, the linguistic behaviour of their peers and the official language of instruction begin to determine their choice of language. The third and fourth stages are even more crucial—entry into the work force or an institution of higher learning, and the selection of a mate.[4]

Many students at Macdonald-Cartier want to continue to cultivate their French roots, but because of a massive exposure to English they are already bicultural and may slip into an exclusively English-speaking world through work and marriage. They themselves may continue to speak French, but their children may never learn the language.

Statistics on the loss of French, anglicization of the home, and the predominance of English among rising numbers of mixed-language couples do not bode well. The 1971 census shows there were 737,360 people of French origin in Ontario but only 482,045 of French mother tongue. That is, only two-thirds of the people of French background can still speak French. The remaining third has been assimilated. There are three main areas of Ontario where francophones are concentrated, and loss of the language varies according to region. In the eastern counties near Ottawa, and in the north around Sudbury, over 80 per cent of people of French origin can still speak French. But in the south around Toronto and Niagara, the proportion falls to 45 per cent.[5] The difference is due to the percentage of francophones in each region. In the east and the north, they account for about a quarter of the total population, whereas in the south they represent barely a tenth.[6]

Anglicization, which demographers define as the switch from French to English at home, is a determining factor in the weakening of Franco-Ontarian culture. It is the first step towards total loss of the French language. In Ontario the rate of anglicization is about 30 per cent.[7] Translated into numbers this means that of 482,000 people of French mother tongue, 144,000 have adopted English at home. Of 737,360 people of French origin, only 338,000 — about half — still speak French at home. In areas with high concentrations of francophones, the rate of anglicization is not as high: in Sudbury, for example, it is only 18 per cent. As various researchers point out, statistics for the overall population are misleading because of the rising attraction of English among young people. In the 35–44 age group, where the transfer from one language to another is considered to be permanent, anglicization is 40 per cent for the whole of Ontario and 26 per cent for the Sudbury area.[8]

There are a number of reasons why French is dropped at home. Some francophone couples use English at home at least part of the time because they work in English and feel more comfortable discussing their professional lives in the language. However, French usually disappears as a home language when a francophone marries an anglophone. In Ontario mixed marriages are becoming more and more common. Among francophones of marrying age, one in three marries an anglophone and stops using French at home.[9]

The children of mixed marriages do not always lose their French heritage. But unless French parents insist that their children attend French schools and participate in French cultural activities, the language tends to disappear. When French is not used at home, however, the children do not have enough opportunities to practise the language. More comfortable in English, they will often gravitate as adolescents to a completely English milieu. Under these conditions, assimilation is delayed, but not stopped, for one generation.

The social factors that contribute to assimilation are many and complex. The most important are without doubt the break-down of self-enclosed Franco-Ontarian communities and the shift of the population to urban centres.[10] In the past, people were cut off from the influences of industry and the consumer society, both of which operated in English. Now the French minority continually encounters English at work, at political meetings, and through the media. Urbanization, which has resulted in the mixing of French and English populations, has also been accompanied by greater religious tolerance. French Catholics are now willing to marry not only Irish Catholics but also English Protestants.

Where the French population is dense, English has less influence. Anglicization is low in Cochrane county in the north, for example, which is almost 50 per cent French-speaking. However, many people do not want to stay in the north or the east, where preservation of French is more assured. Instead, they are drifting to Toronto, Hamilton, and London in southern Ontario, where job opportunities are more plentiful and exciting, but where French is the home language of only a tiny percentage of the population.[11]

In 1941 only 12 per cent of the French in Ontario lived in the southern region. By 1971 26 per cent of Franco-Ontarians lived there.[12] Services in French—schools, churches, and community activities—are so few and far between in southern Ontario, and English influences so overwhelming, that Ottawa's French daily newspaper, *Le Droit*, has referred to the area as "*les fours crématoires des franco-ontariens*," the crematoria of the Franco-Ontarians.

Assimilation can be explained by other factors as well. The English majority is not interested in promoting institutional bilingualism or allowing the French community to develop separate educational and social organizations. This attitude contrasts sharply with that of New Brunswick, where the provincial government has given the French community its own school boards. Many francophones in Ontario—particularly those who have migrated south—are not willing to spend their lives fighting for recognition of French in public life. They retain sentimental attachments to their French heritage but will not make the effort to pass it on to their children.

The motivation of Franco-Ontarians to preserve their culture is also undermined by the attitudes of some Quebecers who make Franco-Ontarians feel embarrassed about the quality of their French. Many francophones in Quebec consider the French in Ontario contaminated by the English, regarding them as hybrids rather than authentic francophones. Historian Pierre Savard of the University of Ottawa describes the double bind of Franco-Ontarians: "From a feeling of shame and a refusal of one's identity, to cultural transfer and acculturation, there is often only a step. One needs a large dose of confidence or recklessness to identify with a group that is considered to be negligible in one's own province, and sometimes looked down upon from outside, as was the case during the Superfrancofête in Quebec."[13]

Minorities often complain that they are the helpless victims of the cultural tidal waves that sweep them away. However, assimilation is sometimes the conscious choice of individuals who find their cultural group stifling. Mordecai Richler has become a controversial figure in the Jewish community of Montreal because his novels describe this process of conscious assimilation. Richler writes vividly of the dilemma of the children of Jewish immigrants who struggle to free themselves from the restrictions of their cultural group and find a place for themselves in the broader North American society.

Cultures compete with one another for followers, but the strongest strains do not always win. In Montreal and Quebec City there are American-born professors in the French universities who have thrown themselves so whole-heartedly into the culture of French Quebec that they refuse to speak English. Some have become ardent Quebec nationalists and are bringing up their children completely in French. One anglophone in Sudbury who usually identifies more with French than English culture is Robert Dickson, professor of French-Canadian literature at Laurentian University. He participated in Franco-Ontario's Quiet Revolution in the 1970s and continues to be active in the French community. In Ontario, however, people such as Dickson are rare: the cultural pull is usually in the other direction.

Many young Franco-Ontarians find the French community is not sufficiently dynamic or creative to allow them to develop their potential. They find the philosophy of *la survivance*, which is still an important force in the community, irrelevant or depressing, and want nothing to do with it. They read English magazines and newspapers that reflect their preoccupations, not *Le Voyageur* with its Catholic tone and its concern for French rights. The cultural awakening that began in the late 1960s excited many young people of the time because the plays, poetry, and songs that emerged reflected their concerns. Today, however, cultural expression in Franco-Ontario cannot easily compete with North American films, theatre, and books.

Some of the older generation also find the French community suffocating. Retired Inco miner Albert Ouellet, who was born in Cabano, Quebec, considers the cultural elite of Sudbury closed to working-class people like himself. The English community, he says, offers him more room to manoeuvre. "I'm a French Canadian. There's no question about that," he pointed out. "But in certain places, I'm more accepted by the English than the French." For many years, Ouellet was active in the Mine-Mill union. Always a persuasive speaker, he has become popular at a toastmaster's club in Sudbury. "I'm the only miner in the group and the only French Canadian, but if the organization were French, I wouldn't be accepted."

Quebec could probably draw the francophone communities across Canada into its cultural orbit if its television, radio, films, and magazines were more open and pluralistic in their vision of the world. As it is, the French in Quebec consider that francophones in the rest of Canada have no future. When the subject comes up, they say the French outside Quebec are dying off, and that they are tainted by their contacts with the English.

At this juncture of French / English relations in Canada, it is difficult to interpret correctly the meaning of statistics on assimilation in Franco-Ontario. The percentage of people of French mother tongue is diminishing: in 1941, it was 7.6 per cent; in 1971, 6.3 per cent; and in 1976, 5.7 per cent.[14] But these statistics do not necessarily mean that the Franco-Ontarian minority is doomed to disappear. Historian Pierre Savard points out that the will of Franco-Ontario to survive and flourish compensates for a diminishing population.[15] This desire manifests itself not only in cultural expression, but also in pressure upon the provincial government for official recognition of French and the expansion of French services.

Another factor that favours French is the importance that the language has assumed over the past ten years in Canadian society. In spite of the ambivalent feelings they express, members of the English elite across the country consider that bilingualism at an individual level is becoming more and more necessary. Anglophones perceive that official bilingualism in the federal government and the vigour of Quebec are not passing phenomena. It is now accepted that French is required for certain jobs, and interest in French immersion programs is spiralling. In Sudbury, for example, over 1,500 English children in the elementary schools were enrolled in French immersion programs in 1982. Robert

Bradley, superintendent of French immersion for the Sudbury Board of Education, predicts that by 1987, one-third of all English elementary school children will be in the stream. "Immersion is so popular," he said, "that couples who are planning to have children are calling the board to find out where future immersion schools will be located so they can buy a home in the right neighbourhood."

Bilingualism is making progress among the English in Ontario. Ontarians of French mother tongue account for less than 6 per cent of the population, but over 10 per cent of the total population can speak French.[16] The new status of French among the English elite enhances the legitimacy of the Franco-Ontarian minority. In the long run, it could dampen the fires of assimilation that some francophones feel are now out of control.

Part III

People of the Frontier

While *la survivance* is part of the thinking of every Franco-Ontarian, it is not the only leitmotiv of Nouvel-Ontario culture. The heart of the community lies in the spirit of the frontier—in the adventurous ways of a people who want to explore the world and create new things. This innovative spirit is everywhere. It is reflected in the cultural realm by Sudbury theatre coach Hélène Gravel, who inspires students at Macdonald-Cartier high school to write prize-winning plays. It is found in playwright Robert Marinier, painter Luc Robert, *chansonnier* Robert Paquette, and book publisher Gaston Tremblay.

Yet the frontier spirit of Nouvel-Ontario shows itself most strongly in the world of labour and business, where unexpected developments—dramatic, often historic actions—are part of the legend of the community. The miners of Sudbury who work for Inco and Falconbridge, the lumber barons of Hearst, Timmins, and Dubreuilville, financiers Robert Campeau and Paul Desmarais: these are some of the people who have broken new ground in the fields of labour and business. They are not always given proper recognition or credit by the community's cultural elite, but they are as creative, as dynamic—and as French—as the playwrights, poets, and *chansonniers*. Their achievements form an integral part of the culture of Nouvel-Ontario.

Chapter 7

At the turn of the century, even a bit before
off trains
from Trois-Rivières, Montréal
Lac St-Jean, Québec, the Gaspé,
they came.

Overalls pockets cold and penniless and empty
but for a few words of "anglais"
Overalls hearts still warmed
by memories of wood-stove fires in kitchens
at family gatherings.

And as soon
as their broken down boots
touch the land
shuffled off
with hardhats, picks, shovels and compasses
and then down the hole
a few or many hundreds of feet under the earth
to that under-day, under-world, under-life
with its always night and cold and damp
and that taste of dust tugging at their mouths
and that lingering echo of pain in the stone
is the leftover shriek of this guy
pinned in a corner yesterday
by a derailed orecar.
. . . .

Our history
is this story
the story of these faces
of these arms
of these hearts
of this tongue ...

Jean-Marc Dalpé, "L'histoire, la nôtre," 1980[1]

Unsung Heroes of
the Labour Movement

As he stood up to face the Burkett commission[2] on mine safety, Jacques Gignac was calm and self-assured under the gaze of the commissioners seated on the stage. This was a meeting of two different worlds.

The commissioners were bureaucrats. They belonged to a world of committee meetings and official reports, and looked as though they could not lift anything heavier than a briefcase. Written on their faces was the tentative look of people who have always worked behind desks in offices.

Gignac was a miner, with a strident step and a determined jaw. A former union president with strong roots in the French community, he was at home in the rough domain of unions and mines. The controversial bonus system of payment for miners was what Gignac had come to discuss. Wearing a leather jacket, jeans, and boots, his hair creeping down to his shoulders, he looked strikingly different from the commissioners in their pin-striped suits.

The Burkett commission met in Sudbury, the nickel capital of North America, in the fall of 1980 to find out why there were so many accidents and deaths in the mines. Under scrutiny were International Nickel Company of Canada (Inco) and Falconbridge Mines, the two companies that have made Sudbury famous.

The city has prospered under their rule, but it has also suffered. Misshapen black hills without a tree or a blade of grass bear down upon the city like ominous clouds. The landscape is bleak. When American astronauts were training for their first moon shots, they went to Sudbury, because the terrain there was the closest scientists could find to that of the moon. Although the city has oases of trees, it looks as though it has dug itself into a great crater. The mammoth ore deposits of the Sudbury basin, and the mines that run beneath them, rule the city like a tyrant that can never be appeased.

Across the barren landscape, for about forty-five kilometres around Sudbury, lonely headframes, like distant grain elevators on a prairie, mark mine shafts plunging a kilometre and more into the earth. Inco's massive smelter looms like a fortress on the outskirts of the city in the old town of Copper Cliff. From the bowels of the smelter rises Sudbury's most famous landmark—the 1,250-foot smoke stack that pollutes the atmosphere and creates acid rain for hundreds of kilometres around. Facing the highway on a hill outside Copper Cliff, huge caldrons of molten rock spill over a smouldering slag heap.

Sudbury was not always like this. At the turn of the century, the city was as beautiful as a Lawren Harris painting, with gentle pines, majestic rocks, and clear lakes. In the valley, where the French had farms, wheat, hay, and corn grew in abundance. According to old-timers, thousands of horses once grazed in the fields. Then the lumber barons cut down the forests and the mining companies built open smelters in the fields. Sulphur fumes burned the crops and grass; erosion washed away what was left, leaving pock-marked hills of charred rock. As the companies expanded, more and more mines opened. Death and accidents on the job became part of the cycle of life. Like the fishing communities in Newfoundland, families in Sudbury resigned themselves to the possibility that one day their men might go to work and never return.

The nickel companies form the economic backbone of Sudbury, but the miners give the city its character. The story of the miners is closely linked to the legend of the International Union of Mine, Mill, and Smelter Workers, popularly known as Mine-Mill. Part of a working-class movement that swept the United States and Canada during the first half of the century, Mine-Mill's struggle captured the imagination of progressive people across the continent.

The French miners did not always figure so prominently in the union, but in the end they contributed an important chapter to Canadian labour history by saving Mine-Mill from absorption by the United Steelworkers of America. Although not widely recognized, the French were the soul of an historic fight to save one of Canada's most avant-garde and controversial unions from passing into oblivion.

Founded at the turn of the century under the name Western Federation of Miners (WFM), Mine-Mill is one of the most colourful and militant unions in North American history. The idea of the union was born in an Idaho jail after an unsuccessful strike at a mine in 1892. Thrown into jail on a trumped-up charge, the miners decided to fight atrocious conditions in the mines with a tough grass-roots union. Ten years later, the WFM had gathered together many small independent unions from mining camps in the United States and Canada.

According to retired Sudbury miner Jim Tester, who is compiling a history of Mine-Mill, "miners moved quite freely from camp to camp, north and south, east and west. The whole of North America was their stamping ground: the Western Federation of Miners was their union. It was an international organization in the real sense."

The WFM, and its successor, Mine-Mill, was always in conflict with the mainstream of the labour movement and society at large. Dissatisfied with the status quo, it advocated changes in the power structure of the North American economy. Initially a member of the American Federation of Labor, the WFM decided that the AFL's policies were too conservative and formed the Western Labor Union and, later, the Industrial Workers of the World. Fifty years later, Mine-Mill in Canada locked horns with the Canadian Congress of Labor (CCL) and the Co-operative Commonwealth Federation (CCF), the predecessor of the New Democratic Party. Both the CCL and the CCF felt Mine-Mill was too radical.

The Western Federation of Miners started in Canada around 1895, in the coal mines of British Columbia. In 1916 it changed its name to the International Union of Mine, Mill, and Smelter workers, to describe more accurately its jurisdiction. Ontario locals sprouted up in northern Ontario after 1905. The first Sudbury local was set up in 1913 at the Garson mine, but it didn't last long. After the First World War, mine shut-downs were common and employers tried to smash the union. Disunity among union members played in their favour: people were torn between Mine-Mill and the newer and more radical One Big Union movement. By 1925, Mine-Mill was gone, and for the following ten years the union scene in northern Ontario was quiet.[3]

Conditions in the mines continued to be deplorable. During the Depression, miners in Sudbury worked up to twelve hours a day, seven days a week for as little as $1.75 a day. Rather than pay the stiff twenty-five-cent streetcar fare, people walked to work. William Kon describes what the mines were like in *Boom Town Into Company Town*:

> You either go to the mine or the smelter. It doesn't matter which because they both rate near the top for accidents and near the bottom for insurance risks. In the mines the loose nickel oxidizes and the heat rises in wet, steamy clouds. And when you drive a shovel all day into rock that is heavy with ore, the water drips from your body and in two weeks your clothes rot from never being dry. And if you stay there long enough the dust goes in your lungs and forms scabs and one day you stop breathing. This is technically known as silicosis. But you really don't have to worry about that too much. Every six months you get another medical examination. If you look a little rocky, they find they are overstaffed for the time and you are laid off.[4]

In the mid-1930s, Mine-Mill resurfaced in Sudbury, Kirkland Lake, and Timmins. A turning point came with the great Kirkland Lake gold mine strikes of 1941–42. The issue was union recognition. Although the miners lost, the strike resulted in federal legislation guaranteeing workers the right to form a union and negotiate collectively. This encouraged Mine-Mill organizers in Sudbury to open an office. The mining companies tried to stop the union from making any headway. Former union president Jim Tester, in his booklet *The Shaping of Sudbury—A Labour View*, describes what the companies did:

> On February 24, 1942, under the leadership of a certain Harry Smith, superintendent of the Frood mine, twelve stope bosses came down as a body to the union hall. Armed with pickaxe handles, they proceeded to smash furniture, break windows, and scatter records on the floor

and into the street. They beat up the two union organizers present there so badly, they had to be sent to the hospital. Surprisingly, nobody was arrested. All the strong-arm squad were officially "at work" in the mine!

A former union officer told me that when he saw Jack Whelahan, one of the beaten men, lying in a hospital bed, he didn't recognize him. "His face was like an old piece of liver," he said.

No doubt it was thought that such acts of terror would frighten workers from the union. In the long run, it had exactly the opposite effect. The company taught the union leaders a lesson they would not forget in a hurry. They changed their organizational strategy. From an open public approach, they went to a home-by-home campaign. They concentrated on the various ethnic communities, using volunteer organizers who were known and trusted by those communities. A secret sign-up campaign was launched. A leaflet was printed shortly after the violent assault on the union office. Ten thousand copies were distributed, door-to-door, throughout Sudbury Basin communities. At night, of course.[5]

To counteract Mine-Mill, Inco spent thousands of dollars promoting a company union which the miners called Nickel Rash; it got nowhere. In 1944 Mine-Mill signed contracts with Inco and Falconbridge and moved like wildfire to establish a network of locals throughout north-eastern Ontario. In Sudbury, Mine-Mill was now a power to be reckoned with and Bob Carlin, president of its local 598, was a hero. His popularity was so widespread that Sudbury elected him to the Ontario legislature on the CCF ticket in 1943, a year before the contracts with Inco and Falconbridge were signed.

Labour unity did not last long. A conflict broke out between certain CCFers and the leftists in Mine-Mill. Carlin was labelled a communist and eventually dismissed from the CCF. Critical of its leftist leadership, the Canadian Congress of Labor in 1949 expelled Mine-Mill. The union, however, was strong enough to operate on its own. Insisting upon complete independence, the Canadian locals of Mine-Mill broke away from the American parent union in 1955.[6]

In the 1960s—after more than fifty years of historic action—Mine-Mill collapsed as a coast-to-coast Canadian union. In Sudbury, the Inco division of the union was smashed by virulent anti-communists in the Canadian Labor Congress[7] and the United Steelworkers of America, with help from the churches, the newspapers, the nickel companies, and the mayor. After years of systematic raids, the Inco workers joined the American union in 1962. Five years later the National Office of Mine-Mill called a special merger convention where the majority of the other locals across Canada also voted to join the Steelworkers. The Falconbridge workers, however, refused to follow suit. They contested the merger vote in the courts until it reached the Supreme Court of Canada. Fiercely independent, and proud of their history as one of the most democratic and progressive unions in Canada, the Falconbridge workers of Mine-Mill local 598 won their right to stand alone in 1968. Today, they still do not belong to a union federation. In 1969, once the dust had settled in Sudbury, local 598 helped found the Council of Canadian Unions, with Kent Rowley and Madeleine Parent.[8] But in 1974 it had a falling out with the council and withdrew.

What was it about the Falconbridge workers that made them cling so tenaciously to Mine-Mill? The answer lies with the French miners who formed the majority at Falconbridge. Like their confrères in Quebec at the Confederation of National Trade Unions, which is controlled by Quebecers, they wanted a home-grown union, not an American operation controlled from afar by union bureaucrats. As a minority which was always fighting to be heard, this was important. The Steelworkers, they believed, would swallow them up.

Jacques Gignac, at 33, is too young to have fought in the bitter Mine-Mill battle against the Steelworkers that tore Sudbury apart in the fifties and sixties. His father, however, was a Mine-Miller, and Gignac remembers that as a child he refuted charges made by the priests at school that Mine-Mill was an evil union run by Communist Party atheists. He comes out of a fierce tradition of independence that marks the miners of the French community.

Gignac was the last witness to appear before the Burkett commission on mining safety during its hearings in the fall of 1980. His appearance was unexpected. For two years he had been president of Mine-Mill. Then, in 1979, he was defeated by Emile Prud-homme, an older Franco-Ontarian miner with a longer history in the union. Gignac was not appearing before the commission on behalf of the union; rather, he was taking a position contrary to it. He had been a controversial president, and some people in the union were not pleased to see him testify.

Gignac was invited to the hearings by the commission chairman, who had heard he had important things to say about the bonus scheme of payment for miners. The bonus system is a piece-work system whereby miners get a basic salary plus a bonus for productivity. The official view of both Mine-Mill and the Steelworkers was that elimination of the bonus system would not necessarily result in fewer accidents.

Gignac disagreed. "The bonus," he told the commission, "is an incentive to break or stretch the rules of safety." He explained that the bonus system pushed miners beyond their physical capacity. The bonus is calculated on the basis of the productivity of the team. Because older miners did not want to let down their teammates, they often took risks that resulted in accidents.

Later, Gignac talked informally about the disastrous effects of the bonus system on the health of miners. "There are miners in my family," he said, "who are completely burnt out, who can't work anymore. An uncle of mine is in hospital now. His heart has given out. He can hardly walk up a flight of stairs. Another uncle is on permanent disability because of a whole series of injuries that have ruined him. He suffers from 'white hands.' After continuous exposure to the vibration of the drills, the hands break down and the muscles can't grip. Miners destroyed by their work know what has happened to them. But they're proud. They won't admit they've been exploited. Instead, they reminisce about former days when they could work at super-human levels."

It took courage for Gignac to go against both unions and recommend elimination of the bonus system. Although some miners supported Gignac's view, others—particularly the younger miners—like the system because they can make great sums of money on it. Gignac maintained that the principle behind the bonus system is wrong because it exploits and eventually damages workers. When the Burkett commission published its report in April 1981, it recommended that the bonus system be changed to reflect the productivity of all miners rather than focusing upon each team of miners. This, they felt, would take the pressure off individual miners. In Gignac's view, implementation of this recommendation would have been a big step forward; however, it was rejected by the mining companies and the unions.

Like many French miners in Sudbury, Gignac has roots that go back to the rural communities of Franco-Ontario. His father ran a farm in the town of St. Charles, but left for a job at Inco because he couldn't make enough to feed his family. His grandfather worked as a lumberjack in Chapleau. "My grandfather died on the job of pneumonia," Gignac said. "He was told he'd lose his job if he didn't come to work, so he chopped trees until he dropped."

Although the miners are proud to be French, they do not see eye-to-eye with the traditional French elite. For Gignac, the teachers, Jesuits, and professionals—even the people at the Centre des jeunes and the theatre—live in a different world. In the early 1970s, playwright André Paiement wrote plays about the world of miners and lumberjacks, but his productions were not well received by the miners of Sudbury. The ambiance of the Théâtre du Nouvel-Ontario with its Collège du Sacré-Coeur roots and hard-rock music was foreign to them.

Whenever intellectuals and working class from the French community mix, tensions surface. When Gignac was president of Mine-Mill between 1977 and 1979, some French students from Laurentian University interviewed him for a film they were making on the French community. "They were looking for French heroes, but I disappointed them," he said. "Although I speak French, I did most of my union business in English. They didn't understand a point I was making in French, so I said: 'Look, I'll explain it in English.' That turned them off."

In Franco-Ontario there has always been a sharp division between the elite and the working class, a division that is less pronounced in Quebec. In the forties and fifties, for example, educated people in Quebec such as Madeleine Parent and Jacques Perrault became deeply involved in the union movement. This did not happen among the French in Sudbury. In the fifties, when Mine-Mill in Sudbury decided to publish half its union paper in French, it went to Quebec to find a writer in the union movement for the job. The position was accepted by Gilles Hénault, a poet, journalist, and union activist who worked alongside Madeleine Parent and Kent Rowley during some of the trying textile strikes in Quebec in the late 1940s and early 1950s. The renowned Collège du Sacré-Coeur in Sudbury was turning out graduates who could have done the job, but they were not interested in the miners' world.

In Quebec an individual such as Jacques Gignac would probably be friendly with the French intellectuals, but in Sudbury the educated elite is too conservative for these kinds of associations. The Franco-Ontarian intellectuals define the community principally in terms of language and culture. Unlike their counterparts in Quebec, they have not tried to give the working class an adequate social framework. The one exception to this in Franco-Ontario are the activists in the co-operative movement, who stopped financial exploitation by the loan companies of the working class and the rural population, by creating a network of *caisses populaires*.

Although they form the core of life in Sudbury, the miners live in a world of their own. More than the university people or the professionals, they are deeply attached to Sudbury. The mines and forests—the very rock and soil of Nouvel-Ontario—is in their blood. Yet the media, schools, and cultural institutions are run by people who take little interest in their lives. Radio-Canada programming, for example, does not reflect their world. This gulf between the working class and the traditional elite works against the broad interests of the French in Sudbury. Until the social and political leadership recognizes the importance of the miners, many feel the community will never be able to develop the way it should.

Because the French middle class keeps its distance, the miners are often more loyal to their work and their union than to their culture. This attitude was poignantly reflected in a Radio-Canada television series on the French community in Sudbury, presented by Montreal journalists in January 1978. Gignac was asked whether he saw himself first and foremost as a francophone. There was a long pause. "I've never really thought about it," he said. Finally, he replied that he saw himself first as a socialist and then as French. This remark did not go unnoticed by certain Jesuits and other members of the cultural elite who labelled him a heretic.

If the miners dismiss the social and political leadership of their community, it is largely because they feel they have been betrayed by it in the past. In the fifties and sixties, when the miners were fighting for Mine-Mill against the Steelworkers, they received no support from the clergy, professionals, or university teachers. In fact, this elite group did everything it could to destroy the union. The priests condemned Mine-Mill from the pulpit and terrorized the miners' children in the schools with diatribes against the union. The University of Sudbury, the successor to the Collège du Sacré-Coeur, even set up a course on unions which was designed to discredit Mine-Mill and to provide moral and organizational support for the rival Steelworkers.

Some Mine-Mill leaders in Sudbury were members of the Communist Party. However, most miners did not feel that this fact affected their ability to lead the union. In the thirties and forties, those most committed to organizing tough industries such as mining were often Communist Party members. Finns, Ukrainians, and Poles in the union rank-and-file were often communist sympathizers. During the fifties, at the height of the anti-communist witch-hunts led by Senator Joseph McCarthy in the United States, affiliation with the party became suspect and the Canadian Congress of Labor expelled all unions believed to have Communist Party links.

The French miners refused to be influenced by the witch-hunts going on around them. They themselves were not communists, but they judged their leaders on their union record, not their personal politics. A sense of working-class consciousness, which was a strong part of the Mine-Mill tradition, bound the miners together. The French community's leaders refused to listen to the miners and eventually lost their allegiance.

The clergy never understood the nature of the miners' feelings about their work and their union. Mining is tough, and the miners have always fought hard to improve their working conditions. In spite of this, they like their work. For them, mining is a way of life, not simply a job. The union is part of this life. Working together for common goals has forged a strong sense of solidarity among the miners—so strong that, for many miners, the union is second only to their families.

Miner Lauré St-Jean led the last stage of Mine-Mill's determined fight to beat off the Steelworkers at Falconbridge and keep local 598 in Sudbury alive. A tough muscular man with a soft voice and a steady eye, St-Jean has worked over thirty years in the mines. Although everyone who works underground is called a miner, the real miners are those like St-Jean who work in the dark with drills and dynamite, blasting ore in the stopes. The stopes are huge underground caverns formed when ore is removed from around a mine shaft. The jobs in these areas are the most exhausting and dangerous. Black as a dungeon, damp, dusty, and hot, ringing with ear-splitting noise, the stope is the front-line of the mine. All the other mine workers—tram loaders, welders, electricians and pipe fitters—are there to support the miners in the stope.

"We work in teams in the stope," explained St-Jean. "It's dangerous, so we must rely upon one another. We must be close." St-Jean talked with pride about miners' skills and the constant difficulties they face. In trying to explain the special bonds that exist between miners, he referred to a mining congress he once attended in Hungary. "Miners there have their own anthem. When they meet, they shake hands and say 'good luck!' We don't have an anthem but we have the same feeling about our work and our team-mates."

Mine-Mill was important to the French miners because it made more effort than any other institution in Sudbury to recognize their needs. Until the late 1930s, the French found it difficult to get employment in the mines. Once they had jumped that hurdle, they suffered from blatant discrimination on the job. This stopped only when Mine-Mill came to Sudbury.

Retired miner Philias Castonguay described the situation this way. "I joined Inco in 1937," he recalled over a cup of coffee at his farm in Chelmsford, outside of Sudbury. "Until then, we couldn't get in. The companies preferred Ukrainians, Finns, and Poles because they'd take an incredible amount of shit, and because they were bigger. But in the 1930s, Inco did an about face and decided to let us in. We had farms here in the valley, but the crops were dying because of the sulphur from the smelters." Castonguay looked wistfully out of his kitchen window at the vast expanse of grass stretching into the distance. "The companies have cut down on pollution, but even today many crops will not grow.

"My father had a dairy farm in those days, and I drove horses for him. Earlier he had teams of moose." At that point Castonguay's wife brought out some old family pictures showing a team of moose pulling a sleigh. "Some days I could hardly see our neighbours for the smoke. You could actually taste the sulphur fumes. Pressure was building up against the companies because of the ruined crops. Farmers had no hay for their cattle. This used to be an area rich with grain, corn, and hazel nuts. All that disappeared with the smelters. Trees died from the top down.

"Finally the priests got together and made a deal with Inco. They decided to sacrifice the farming communities in the valley for jobs in the mines. *Ils nous ont vendus comme des moutons!* They sold us like sheep!" Castonguay banged the table with his fist, and then shrugged. "Like hundreds of other young French Canadians here in the valley, I got into Inco with a letter from my priest. I could never have had a job without it. That," he said, "was the beginning of the terrible alliance between the French priests and Inco. Even then, the discrimination did not end. In the mines the bosses called us 'pea crackers' and 'frogs.' When they heard us speaking French, they told us to 'speak white.' That stopped with the arrival of Mine-Mill. The union leaders ordered the bosses to cut it out."

Outside of the mine and the union, however, Sudbury treated the French like non-persons. Bell Telephone, for example, openly discriminated against them. In the 1950s, operators were forbidden to use French on the telephone lines. Quebec writer Gilles Hénault recalled an unsettling experience he had with Bell when he lived in Sudbury. "I remember trying to call my mother in Quebec," he said. "At the time all long-distance calls were handled by operators. My mother couldn't speak English, so I asked for a French operator. If my mother picked up the phone and heard English, she'd think it was the wrong number and would hang up. The operator explained that she was French, but that Bell would not let her use the language. She called Quebec, spoke English, and my mother hung up."

Most institutions in Sudbury tried to pretend the French didn't exist, but Mine-Mill made it a policy to recognize French where they could. By today's standards, the union did not go far enough. Although many shop stewards were French, until the 1960s the union leadership was mainly English. Because of this, union meetings for the full membership took place exclusively in English. But in the forties and fifties, when French was systematically ignored outside of Quebec, Mine-Mill behaved in an exemplary manner. For example: in predominantly French areas such as Chelmsford, district meetings were always held in French. In addition, the union newspaper and information leaflets were always published in both languages. "It meant a great deal to the French miners that half the paper was in French," noted Gilles Hénault, who handled the publication in the early 1950s. Hénault also did a daily French radio program called *Clément et Clémentine*, which always carried union news.

Though Mine-Mill's French membership was confined to the Sudbury local, the national edition of the union paper also had a French section. It was edited by Montreal union activist Danielle Dionne, who travelled to Mine-Mill's head office in Toronto each month to prepare the material. Madeleine Parent, the militant French union organizer from Montreal who worked with textile workers, frequently visited Mine-Mill in Sudbury. She maintained close links with the union because of its grass-roots orientation and its insistence upon Canadian autonomy. Parent's goals for the labour movement were similar to those of Mine-Mill and she frequently collaborated with the union's leaders. "The French were very comfortable in Mine-Mill," she said. "Because they had bilingual publications and their own union hall where they could speak French, they felt Mine-Mill was their union."

In the late 1950s, when the Steelworkers started their huge campaign to conquer Mine-Mill, francophones in the union became more active. The French were slow to become union leaders because they thought they spoke poor English and had less education than other workers. The employers were English, so the French miners let the English unionists be the leaders. Naturally, the English were quite happy to go along with this approach. The French began to rise to the top only after leading the grass-roots movement to keep Falconbridge, the last strong-hold of the union, from the Steelworkers. At that point their leadership talents, which had always been seriously underestimated, were finally recognized.

One of the first francophones to play a dynamic role in Mine-Mill was Albert Ouellet. In the 1940s he organized campaigns for former union president Bob Carlin when he ran for the Ontario legislature. By the late 1950s, Ouellet was a shop steward. A wiry man with flashing eyes and a rapier wit, Ouellet is now retired. Like Philias Castonguay, he entered the mines in 1937 with a letter from his priest.

"We all wanted jobs in the mines," he recalled, "but the conditions were terrible. I started shovelling rock at the Levack mine for forty cents an hour, seven days a week. There were no days off and no holidays. We were all French there. Every day people were fired. The superintendent would look down from the hill and fire about thirty-five men, just to show who was boss.

"I did every job you could imagine. I worked in the rock house separating nickel from the rock by hand, I was a car loader, and I was an underground rock crusher. Finally I became a drill fitter because I was good with machines. For a while my wife and I ran a little grocery store at the Levack railway station to supplement our meagre income. We called it Dogpatch," he laughed. It looked like something out of the cartoon strip *Li'l Abner*. Levack was a hill-billy place—all French—just a bunch of broken-down shacks.

"In 1943 I decided Levack was no place for kids, so I applied to get a job at Murray Mine, which was opening up near Sudbury. The superintendent at Levack didn't want to let me go. Luckily he got a dose of some mysterious disease and went to the hospital. Another superintendent took over—that's how I got my transfer," he recalled. "The first time I heard union talk was at Murray Mine. The Finns, Yugoslavs, Ukrainians, and Poles started the union, but the French quickly became strong supporters."

According to Ouellet and other old-timers, Mine-Mill filled a tremendous gap in the lives of the French miners. "There were two things that really made a difference," said Ouellet. "One was the union halls where we could meet and socialize in French. The other was the summer camp for the kids. The French," he explained, "were the poorest people in Sudbury. Miners' wages were low and families were large. Moulin à Fleur was nothing but slums. Where else," he asked, "could we find such a camp? The church wasn't offering any such thing."

To run the camp, Mine-Mill employed a full-time recreation director, Weir Reid, who also brought in plays, ballets, and singers at a time when Sudbury had little entertainment. Some of the entertainers were left-wingers barred from the American entertainment circuit during the McCarthy witch-hunts. Reid also organized local theatre productions, ballet classes, painting, boxing, and hockey for children and adults. The recreation program was part of a community-oriented policy which reflected the tradition of social consciousness started by Mine-Mill's predecessor, the Western Federation of Miners.

110

By the 1950s Mine-Mill local 598, with its 15,000 members, was bigger than most northern Ontario towns and more influential than any other institution in Sudbury—including the Roman Catholic church. According to the French miners, this made the church uneasy. Philias Castonguay echoed the feelings of many when he said: "The church had a rival. The priests didn't like it, and they decided to find a way to run it out of town."

The church was not the only organization that viewed Mine-Mill with alarm. Inco feared its communist leanings, and the Canadian Labor Congress worried that Mine-Mill would join with other militant unions to become a rival. On the fringes—waiting to pounce—was the United Steelworkers of America. Ever since Mine-Mill had been expelled from the CLC, the Steelworkers had regarded the union as fair game for raiding. Local 598 with its huge membership was a plum: if the Steelworkers could capture the heart of the union in Sudbury, they calculated, the other locals across Canada would fall into their hands like ripe fruit.

Mine-Mill's first strike was a disastrous blow for the union. In 1958 Inco was faced with a loss of contracts and rapidly rising inventories. By the time the company came to the bargaining table, it had already laid off 1,000 workers. It refused even to make a wage offer. Mine-Mill responded with a three-month-long strike that ended in a humiliating contract. Some members turned against the leadership because of the contract; others were dissatisfied for another reason. Because the leaders were constantly under attack from outsiders for their communist leanings, they were unusually sensitive to criticism from within the union. When members presented alternative proposals at meetings, for example, they were often ridiculed or ignored. After a while, those who did not agree with the executive stopped participating. Many members felt a change in leadership would be good for Mine-Mill. The Steelworkers took this opportunity to launch a $2 million campaign against Mine-Mill that kept Sudbury in turmoil for ten years.

The Steelworkers set up shop in Sudbury after the strike in 1958 and started to worm their way into Mine-Mill. Their strategy was to use the Mine-Mill election of 1959 to divide the union. Working upon Mine-Mill's most dissatisfied members, they persuaded some miners who were openly sympathetic to the Steelworkers to run for office. The Steelworkers hoped this group would win and, in a later recertification vote, eventually deliver the entire Mine-Mill local to their union. Don Gillis led the so-called reform slate against former president Mike Solski and a team that was fiercely loyal to Mine-Mill. This marked the beginning of two rival camps within the union.

Albert Ouellet, a member of the Solski team, recalled what the atmosphere was like in Sudbury at the time. "At the time I ran," he said, "everyone was against Mine-Mill—Inco, the newspapers, the CCF, and all the churches. At one point Inco held a meeting with all the important people in Sudbury. The company told this august gathering that if they would defeat Mine-Mill, Inco would support a university."

According to Ouellet, those most committed to running Mine-Mill out of town were the French Catholic priests. "You know," he said, leaning back in a rocking chair in his basement as he told the story, "these days everyone thinks Père Albert Régimbal is a hero." Père Régimbal, a Jesuit who died in 1980, founded the Centre des jeunes; his portrait hangs in Place-Saint-Joseph, the centre's new home. To many he is a saint who promoted the cause of the French. But to the hundreds of French miners who lived through the tumultuous battle between Mine-Mill and the Steelworkers, priests like Albert Régimbal helped destroy a good union. "They were traitors," pronounced Ouellet—a judgment that is shared by many.

"All priests—especially the French ones—were determined to destroy Mine-Mill," he said. "In Sudbury and the valley the priests attacked Mine-Mill from the pulpit." According to Philias Castonguay, priests marched into schools and ripped Mine-Mill buttons from the lapels of school children. "My kids were told I was a communist and they didn't know it. The priest actually threw their Mine-Mill buttons in the waste basket."

Although the miners continued going to church, many stopped contributing. The Sunday collection in Moulin à Fleur's Saint-Jean-de-Brébeuf church dipped from $2,500 to $500 in 1959. "People who had worked hard to build the union felt the priests were shovelling up a helluva lot of bullshit from the pulpit," said Philias Castonguay. "They told the priests what they thought, but they also decided to stop giving to the church."

Supporting the network of French priests discrediting Mine-Mill was Alexandre Boudreau, who gave an adult education course on unions at the Catholic University of Sudbury. An economics professor from the Maritimes who had experience organizing fishing co-operatives, Boudreau was known as a zealous anti-communist. The course, which was aimed directly at miners in Mine-Mill, was part of a strategy to kill Mine-Mill and pave the way for the Steelworkers. Material used in the course came mainly from the Canadian Labor Congress and the Steelworkers. Concentrating on the supposed communist menace in local 598, Boudreau also used literature from the Christian Anti-Communist Crusade, which was inspired by the political teachings of the John Birch Society. As part of the course, Boudreau helped participants organize special committees at the plant level to oppose Mine-Mill at Inco and Falconbridge. To facilitate this, Boudreau secured from some disenchanted Mine-Millers a list of ninety people who had complaints about the union and could be called upon to support an opposition movement.

Although the struggle was between Mine-Mill and the Steelworkers, everyone in the city was involved. At a Catholic social life conference attended by 8,000 people prior to the Mine-Mill election, Archbishop Berry attacked Mine-Mill and mayor Joseph Fabbro said Sudbury was reputed to be a "hotbed of communism for all the North American continent." Fabbro suggested that "if nothing more were gained from this conference, we trust our people will realize the grave responsibility they have in respect to the teachings of communism and remain constantly alert to them."[9]

In 1959 the slate sympathetic to the Steelworkers won the union election and Don Gillis became the new president. Albert Ouellet attributes his personal loss to the priests at St. Anne's church in downtown Sudbury. "Ray Poirier was my opponent," he said, "and he had the total support of the church simply because he was part of the traitorous slate of officers bankrolled by Steel." According to Ouellet, Poirier presented himself as a fine, upstanding man who would, if elected, sweep out communist infiltrators such as Ouellet from Mine-Mill. Ouellet pins the turning point of his election defeat to the events of a particular Sunday at church, events he described with barely contained fury.

"Something very strange was going on at the door of the church just before mass," Ouellet recalled. "A priest was handing out copies of the Catholic magazine published in English by the Irish! Now the French hated the Irish. What's more, English was forbidden in the church. Why was the magazine there?" he asked, leaping out of his chair. "Because," he cried, "it had a story on the front page against Mine-Mill!

"That morning nobody followed the mass. Everyone had his head buried in the article against Mine-Mill. All you could see was a sea of people reading that forbidden magazine. After a while I looked up the aisle and saw crate loads of chocolate bars near the altar. The Knights of Columbus, I found out, were selling them in support of my opponent.

"But the crowning point came during the sermon. The priest got up, and without using my name—but making it clear he was talking about me—told the church my life story. He told them how I had lived in an orphanage in Cabano, Quebec, how I rode the rods during the Depression, and how I finally came to Sudbury. Then he started telling everyone that I'd been to Moscow and that, if elected, I'd be taking my orders from the Russians. He said that anyone who voted for me, or any member of the Mine-Mill slate, would be considered communist and ex-communicated.

"That," Ouellet said, "was the last time I darkened the church door. Until then I'd been active in the church, but I was always considered a nobody because I was a miner. I was making good money—more than a lot of professional people who belonged to that parish—but that didn't count. In addition to my mining job, I worked four hours a day as a carpenter. I offered my services free to Père Régimbal for a carpentry course at his Centre des jeunes. He wouldn't have me—I was just a miner—and what was worse, I was a committed Mine-Miller."

The incident created waves that still affect the Ouellets today. "My two older children, then sixteen and eighteen, were dumbfounded by what took place at church that day. It shook the core of their religious beliefs. From then on, they would have nothing to do with the church. They are now French teachers in Sudbury and Oshawa. My son has an M.A. in French literature from Laval University. Neither will have anything to do with Catholic schools."

With the new slate of officers led by Don Gillis, the anticommunist campaign against the leftists in Mine-Mill spread. The aim of the new leaders was to swing the entire local from Mine-Mill to the Steelworkers through a recertification vote. Red-baiting of former leaders was part of the strategy to discredit the union in the eyes of the members. After the election, recreation director Weir Reid, who was strongly committed to Mine-Mill, was fired by the union executive. Fighting between the two factions in the union broke out at a meeting called to challenge the decision. After the meeting, Poirier got involved in a fist fight and was carried off to the hospital. Poirier later gave a series of interviews to the *Toronto Telegram* in which he labelled Reid a communist agitator. The articles claimed that union members and their families who opposed Reid actually disappeared, while others were intimidated and beaten. Among the headlines over the articles were "Ontario Reds Recruit Seven Year Olds" and "I Learned How to Spread Red Hatred." Reid eventually sued the newspaper and Poirier for defamation and won settlements from both.

As the union battle gathered momentum, there were injunctions against the two factions in Mine-Mill and frequent court hearings. Violent rallies in the Sudbury arena and fist fights in hotel bars became a regular feature of life in the nickel capital. One of the first riots took place when the National Office of Mine-Mill put local 598 under trusteeship to prevent Don Gillis and his executive from further collaborating with the Steelworkers. Armed with a court order, the National Office took over the union hall and barricaded the doors and stairways. The Gillis forces responded by tearing the doors of the hall off their hinges and pinning a home-made hammer-and-sickle flag on the building to convince the crowd that the National Office was communist. Repelled by jets of water from fire hoses, intense fighting broke out between the two factions of the union. Only after the police read the riot act did the crowd disperse. Six thousand miners subsequently signed a petition against Gillis's leadership, but the courts ruled in his favour and returned local 598 to his control.

Shortly after, Gillis organized a mass rally to allow the Canadian Labor Congress and the Steelworkers to address the membership on the merits of leaving Mine-Mill. The National Office members demanded equal time, but Gillis barred them from the meeting. Skirmishes started in the hall before the meeting got under way. Tensions heightened as a group of National Office

115

people, supported by a throng of angry miners, marched on the hall and pushed their way in. "The meeting was supposed to be open to all Mine-Millers, but the police used tear gas to try to prevent us from entering," said Lauré St-Jean, who participated in the march. "The police escorted CLC president Claude Jodoin into the hall for his speech, but Gillis could not call the meeting to order. Chairs were flying and people were fighting." Finally Jodoin left and the meeting broke up when the police ordered everyone to leave the building.

When the Steelworkers saw that rallies were not the way to reach the Mine-Mill members, they resorted to other tactics. Radio, television, and newspapers were asked to lend their support, along with the churches and schools. In addition to approaching people on the job, the Steelworkers stalked bars, hotels, and restaurants popular with the miners. Frequently they tried intimidation. St-Jean remembers the day when a bus-load of Steelworkers from Elliot Lake dropped into the Coulson Hotel to confront a group of committed Mine-Millers at their favourite hang-out. "The Elliot Lake guys roughed up some people, there were fights, then they left."

Everything was leading up to the recertification vote planned by the Steelworkers to challenge Mine-Mill's right to represent the workers at Inco and Falconbridge. In February 1962 the Ontario Labor Relations Board supervised the vote in an atmosphere of tension and suspicion. When the results were finally tallied, the board announced that the Inco workers—though not the workers at Falconbridge—had opted to join the Steelworkers, by a mere fifteen votes over the required majority. The Steelworkers were forced to drop their demand for representation of Falconbridge when numerous forgeries and irregularities in their application for certification came to light. Mine-Mill, however, questioned the validity of the recertification vote at both Inco and Falconbridge. Heated gatherings took place until a second ballot was held in 1965 among Inco workers; it confirmed the Steelworkers' victory. Turmoil did not subside until 1968 when the two unions agreed to end the labour war: the Steelworkers had Inco, but Mine-Mill kept Falconbridge.

The Inco workers' vote to join the Steelworkers, first in 1962 and then in 1965, was the beginning of the end of Mine-Mill as a coast-to-coast union. The Falconbridge miners, however, refused to abandon Mine-Mill, despite subsequent formal raids on their membership by the Steelworkers.

The man who did more than anyone else to keep the miners at Falconbridge from following their colleagues at Inco was Lauré St-Jean. Born in Gatineau, Quebec, and raised in Timmins, St-Jean started off as a lumberjack organizing lumber and sawmill workers in Kapuskasing, Hearst, Iroquois Falls, and Cochrane. Later, after working in the Timmins gold mines, he settled in Sudbury at Falconbridge.

St-Jean became active as a union steward when raiding by the Steelworkers escalated in the early 1960s. He was lated elected vice-president of Mine-Mill at Falconbridge. "We won because we were different from Inco," he explained. "We were much smaller, we had more French people, and we had more committed unionists. There were a lot of fathers and sons, uncles, cousins, and brothers at Falconbridge. We were like a big family. We also had a great proportion of miners. That helped a lot. Miners," he pointed out, "are known for their independent and stubborn spirit. We had the church against us, but that toughened our resolve to stay loyal to the union."

While the French played the most important role in keeping the miners solidly behind Mine-Mill at Falconbridge, the English, Italian, and East European unionists also contributed significantly to the effort. The miners were never divided by language or national origin: their loyalty to one another as miners and Mine-Millers came first.

Mine-Mill was not completely isolated in its fight to survive. It had always had a number of allies. Of these, one of the most prestigious and efficient was undoubtedly Madeleine Parent. During the raids by the Steelworkers, she came to Sudbury to spur on the Mine-Millers. A small woman with impeccable manners and a measured voice, she looks as angelic as a nun, but beneath the tidy exterior is one of the firebrands of the Canadian labour movement. Parent has spent her life in a fierce battle for progressive Canadian unions. With her husband Kent Rowley, she shook traditional Quebec society by leading one of the first strikes at the textile mills in Valleyfield, Quebec, in 1946. Hounded and jailed by then-Quebec Premier Maurice Duplessis, expelled by the American textile unions, she has always worked with the weakest members of the labour force. The Canadian Textile and Chemical

Union, which she helped create, works principally with exploited immigrant women in Toronto, headquarters of the Confederation of Canadian Unions that Parent also helped found in 1969.

Mine-Mill and Madeleine Parent have a long history of mutual support. In 1952 Parent was suddenly fired by the United Textile Workers of America during a strike of 6,000 cotton-mill workers in Montreal and Valleyfield. The union withdrew its support for the strike and brought in new leaders who were ready to sign a contract with the company, Dominion Textile, without even consulting the membership. Parent and Rowley decided to fight back, and the strike went on for another six weeks. Mine-Mill came to the rescue with a strike fund of $1,000 a week and men for the picket line. "We were thrown out of our offices and forced to meet in the fields," said Parent. "When that happened, Mine-Mill sent in a delegation to give us moral support."

After years of fighting for independent Canadian unions in Quebec and Ontario, Parent knew that the Mine-Millers in Sudbury would lose the local control and progressive orientation of their union if they succumbed to the Steelworkers. Addressing huge rallies in both French and English at the peak of the war between the unions, she mesmerized the miners with her force and charisma. "I remember the speeches she used to deliver," recalled miner René Rochon with obvious admiration. "She always got a standing ovation. People went wild when she spoke." Between rallies, Parent went from one French community to another in the valley, talking to miners at small kitchen meetings. Her message was always the same: stick to a Canadian union with a history of progressive action. "Madeleine instructed us as to how the Steelworkers operated and showed us what kind of legal tools we had at our disposal to win out against them," commented Lauré St-Jean. "She convinced us that if we organized ourselves properly we could survive and flourish, even if our leaders deserted us."

The Steelworkers knew Madeleine Parent had tremendous powers of persuasion, so throughout their campaigns to win over the Falconbridge miners they tried to discredit her. One of the pamphlets they circulated described her as "the witch that rode to Sudbury on a red, red, broom." "The Mine-Millers felt badly about that scurrilous leaflet," she recalled. "They thought I might be discouraged from speaking at subsequent meetings. That sort of thing didn't bother me. I was used to the methods of the Steelworkers," she smiled.

Parent says the French miners rallied spontaneously around the idea of keeping their union Canadian. "There was nearly unanimous support among the French for Mine-Mill. Their role in keeping the union from going under in Sudbury has always been underestimated. The French miners had contacts with progressive union people in Quebec and the rest of Canada. They valued autonomy and would not give it up. Other workers were tempted by the large coffers of Steel, but the French felt grass-roots control of the union was more important."

Mine-Mill's problems took an unexpected turn for the worse after the Inco division of local 598 voted to join the Steelworkers for a second time in 1965. The Falconbridge division was still standing firm with Mine-Mill. In 1967, however, the National Office of Mine-Mill in Toronto started holding secret merger talks with the Steelworkers. Some of the national officers had been among the most militant and leftist leaders in Sudbury, but their careers started to look more secure with the Steelworkers, which was offering them jobs. At this point the determination of the Falconbridge workers was put to its most severe test. Lauré St-Jean, who was then vice-president of local 598, suddenly became the key person in the union. Along with many other members, he began to suspect that the union's president, Robin McArthur, was sympathetic to the plans of the National Office. To ensure that Falconbridge would not be drawn into a merger, St-Jean and others set up what they called a Fight for Canadian Unions Committee.

It was this group, led by St-Jean, that master-minded the plan to keep Falconbridge out of the Mine-Mill merger with the Steelworkers. They were willing to lose everything rather than let go of Mine-Mill. Francophone miners formed the majority of the group, which also included some French Mine-Mill loyalists at Inco. One was Albert Ouellet; another was Jean Gagnon, who was working to get compensation for people who developed cancer after working at Inco's sintering plant. Weir Reid, who had been Mine-Mill's recreation director until he was fired by Don Gillis, also participated.

In June 1967 the National Office called all the Mine-Mill locals from across Canada to a special merger convention in Winnipeg. St-Jean, representing local 598, challenged the right of the National Office to even call such a convention. All the other locals, however, voted to join the Steelworkers. The only member from local 598 who voted for the merger was Robin McArthur. By parting company with the Sudbury delegation, he ended his career at local 598. At the next membership meeting in Sudbury, the rank-and-file threw him out as president. "I remember the first meeting we had after the Winnipeg convention," said St-Jean. "Nobody would let McArthur speak. Harvey Murphy from the National Office wanted to present a report on the Winnipeg convention, but people wouldn't let him talk either. Finally, I chaired the meeting."

The National Office branded local 598 a renegade and placed it under trusteeship. The membership decided to fight the decision of the Winnipeg convention, even though it had no union office and no funds. By that time, St-Jean's committee had already hired a lawyer to help the local prepare its case against the National Office and fight the merger. "We knew we had to go right to the Supreme Court to win," said St-Jean, "so we scraped together $10,000 for the case from sales and raffles. For about a year we were in limbo, meeting in basements."

With almost the entire Canadian union movement against them, St-Jean and his group turned to Marcel Pepin, president of the Confederation of National Trade Unions in Quebec. Pepin and the CNTU were already engaged in a series of conflicts with the Steelworkers in Quebec. He sent representatives to Sudbury to give speeches supporting the principles that the French miners in Sudbury wanted to preserve. Madeleine Parent, who by then had moved to Ontario to work with the Canadian Textile and Chemical Union, also went to Sudbury.

Meanwhile, the National Office continued to press the leaders of the rebel committee to drop their court case against them and join the Steelworkers, like all the other Mine-Mill locals across the country. "Nels Thibeault and Harvey Murphy from the National Office never stopped trying to convince us to change our minds," remembered St-Jean. "They would argue with us over dinner at the Coulson Hotel. We drank their booze and ate their food. Then we smiled and told them we'd see them in court. We had no intention of giving up. They were not popular with the membership. When they came to rallies, everyone booed and threw bottles at them. They'd been terrific union leaders in their day, but when people saw that they were supporting Steel just to save their pensions, they turned against them."

In 1968 the Supreme Court of Canada decided that the merger of Mine-Mill with the Steelworkers was valid, but that local 598 could, if it wished, remain independent. Thus ended a twenty-year battle between the two unions that began with the expulsion of Mine-Mill from the Canadian Congress of Labor in 1949. After the Supreme Court decision, all that was left of the historic union that had started with an itinerant band of miners in Idaho was the Falconbridge section of local 598. All the American locals of Mine-Mill had disappeared; the Canadian locals had all joined the Steelworkers.

Since that time, francophones have continued to play important roles in Mine-Mill local 598. It was not until 1974, however, that a Franco-Ontarian miner—Emile Prudhomme—became president of the local. Except for a two-year period when Jacques Gignac was in charge, Prudhomme has run the union ever since. The son of a lumberjack, Prudhomme quit school at sixteen and went to work in the gravel pits in Chelmsford. He first tasted union organizing at the age of eighteen when he tried to start a union at a diamond drilling company. Forced out of the company at age twenty, he joined Falconbridge as a miner in the stope.

Like many other francophones who believed in a grass-roots union, Prudhomme became active in Mine-Mill in the early 1960s when the Steelworkers began raiding. Along with Lauré St-Jean, he was a vice-president of Mine-Mill and a key member of the Committee to Fight for Canadian Unions when the National Office tried to force local 598 into a merger with the Steelworkers. In 1968 he became business agent for the union and, except for brief periods when he went back to the mine, he has worked full-time for Mine-Mill ever since. In the Prudhomme family, the mining tradition is strong: his father started off as a miner in Timmins; two of his sons now work at Falconbridge. Though he has spent a large part of his working life as a union leader and a municipal politician, Prudhomme still sees himself as a miner. Always interested in social questions, he has served as a town councillor in the French county of Rayside-Balfour and as a regional representative for the greater Sudbury region.

Strangely enough, as francophones have risen to positions of influence in the union, formal recognition of the French language has slipped. The union newspaper, for example, is now published in English only, except at election time. Now that the leadership is French, meetings could easily be held in the two languages, but the official language of the union remains English. "French-speaking people who don't understand something at union meetings wait and get an explanation after the meeting is over," said Jacques Gignac. "If they started asking for stuff in French in the middle of a meeting, people would feel they were making a political issue out of French."

This does not necessarily mean that the union is indifferent to the rights of French workers. In 1968 Lauré St-Jean led a union protest against an unexpected ruling by a mining superintendent that English be the exclusive language of work. The union won. Later Prudhomme fought to get signs in the mines in French as well as English. "The Ontario mining act requires that all miners be able to speak English," said Prudhomme. "But there are miners who can speak, but not read English. French signs are important to prevent accidents. I lost on that issue. The company would not spend money for French signs."

The old militancy of the union, however, has clearly faded. Some old-timers feel Mine-Mill is now too tame; others are only too happy to coast along after twenty years of union strife. Jacques Gignac, a committed socialist, brought in new ideas while he was president between 1977 and 1979. However, some Mine-Millers felt he was not sufficiently responsive to the membership. "Gignac was good in many ways," commented one of the younger miners. "He was dynamic and bright, but he made mistakes. However, he could come back."

The French community in Sudbury still bears the scars of the war between Mine-Mill and the Steelworkers. In some families, relatives who supported opposing sides are still not on speaking terms. The church has lost much of its authority with the working class as a result of its stand. Some miners chose to forget what the clergy did; others such as St-Jean, Castonguay, and Ouellet still burn with resentment.

One thing is clear: leading and winning the Mine-Mill campaign at Falconbridge gave the French miners tremendous inner strength. Their victory against almost impossible odds left them feeling confident and secure. Unlike some of Franco-Ontario's intellectuals, they do not wonder who they are and whether they will survive. French miners in Sudbury have unshakeable identities born of their jobs in the mines, their commitment to the union, and their French origins. Some people in the French community consider the miners to be people without culture, but nothing could be further from the truth. To anyone who has spent time in the bar in Mine-Mill hall, in the churches on Sunday, or in the homes of New Sudbury and Moulin à Fleur, the miners give Sudbury much of its character. Without them Sudbury would be just another city.

Chapter 8

the call of the loon
in the light and shadow
of your eyes
and many winter's long nights
  and gusts of North wind
etched deep in the palms
of your hands and on your face

your arms
as large as the trees you bring
  thundering down
your laughter
breaks open the skies
better than that chorus of fat crows
strung along Highway 11
and your heart beats and pumps
to the scream of the "rigodon"

when you dance
your life
the forest, the snow,
  the tears of sweat

you have tamed a land
as mean and hard
as the Devil and yet
when you sing
you are a poet

and your song says
this country is mine.

Jean-Marc Dalpé, Les murs de nos villages, 1980[1]

The Lumber Kings

The tiny lumber town of Dubreuilville lies in one of the most beautiful parts of Nouvel-Ontario: the rocky forest surrounding Lake Superior, immortalized by the Group of Seven painters. At twilight on a wintry Sunday, the town looks like a lost settlement in a dark and silent forest.

The train connecting Dubreuilville to Sault Ste. Marie and Hearst has chugged away. The sawmill on the edge of town is still, the masses have been said, and the hunters have come in from the woods with their deer and partridge. The only sounds are a rippling stream and a cackling of crows. As the light fades, the homes of the lumber workers light up, but rather than looking warm and cosy, they seem small and fragile.

As darkness descends, civilization vanishes and nature takes over. The silence is overwhelming. The spirit of Nouvel-Ontario that the French in the north invoke in their poems, songs, and stories pervades Dubreuilville: wide ethereal skies filled with pale light as the sun rises in the morning ... dark forests that go on forever ... softly stirring animal life pressing in on the edge of the town ... the belief that the true and only season is winter ... the dreams of French pioneers struggling to tame the northern forest.

Franco-Ontarian poet Robert Dickson captures the essence of Nouvel-Ontario in a poem set to music and recorded by CANO-Musique:

Our country is the North
    WHERE
solitude erodes the tender heart
ore of the earth
of rock, forest and cold
    WE
are stubborn and subterranean
in solidarity our stony cries
rise to the four winds
of the possible future

Dubreuilville is isolated in the wilderness, far from any sign of civilization. A steady stream of thundering trailer trucks carry lumber from the sawmill to the United States, but apart from the Algoma Central train which stops only on weekends, there is no public transport. Because of this, most residents own cars.

In spite of the fact that Dubreuilville offers access to an enchanting wilderness of lakes and mountains and streams, a stranger to the town can quickly succumb to claustrophobia because it is so cut off from the usual hustle and bustle of town and city life. After spending four days there, I had an attack of what was clearly cabin fever and decided to leave. For those without cars, the quickest way to leave town is the school bus that takes high school students to Wawa, a larger town seventy kilometres away with a bus service. Since the morning I chose to leave was a school holiday, I hitched a ride 300 kilometres in a lumber truck to Sault Ste. Marie.

Dubreuilville lies outside the most thickly settled part of the French belt of northern Ontario, but it is as French as La Sarre or Rimouski, in Quebec. For Dubreuilville residents, English is the language of *les autres*, out there in the rest of Ontario. Everything in the town—from the sawmill to the elementary school and the police—functions in French. Yet Dubreuilville bears no resemblance to contemporary Quebec. Most of its workers come from Quebec, but when they go home to Abitibi or Lac-Saint-Jean they journey back into the past. The Quebec they know is the Quebec of the 1950s, when the Union Nationale and the clergy dominated the province. Many of the attitudes of the Dubreuilville workers reflect this period. They did not experience the Quiet Revolution or watch the rise to power of the Parti Québécois. "I came to Dubreuilville from Quebec when the town first opened," said one sawmill worker. "A friend of mine worked for the Dubreuils at Magpie. That's how I found out about the place. I go back to Quebec every year to see my family, but it's a Quebec I don't know anymore. I still feel Québécois because my roots are there, but this is my home."

Home, however, is a bit like the planet of Antoine de Saint-Exupéry's *Le petit prince*; it is not quite real. Until a few years ago, Dubreuilville was as closed and inward-looking as a *seigneurie* on the banks of the St. Lawrence. A big gate stretched across the entrance to the road that connects the town and the nearest highway, about thirty kilometres away. A sentinel sat in a trailer beside the gate, keeping out anyone who did not have a pass. Inside the town, there was no police force or municipal government. Residents went in and out as they pleased, but the town was shut to the rest of the world. Although Dubreuilville was part of Ontario, and people there paid their taxes like everyone else, it operated like a fiefdom left over from a by-gone age.

The *seigneurs* were Napoléon Dubreuil and his three brothers, who built the town in 1961 and controlled every aspect of its life. They decreed who could come into the town from the outside. "The place had a very old-fashioned and paternalistic quality to it," said a priest from Sudbury who used to visit. "Even today the Dubreuil family dominates everything in a way that is very unusual."

The Dubreuil brothers are not the only French sawmill owners in the north: they are part of an impressive network of francophone millionaires who control the sawmill industry in Ontario. Along with the Perron brothers of La Sarre who have sawmills in Ontario and Quebec, they dominate the lumber industry east of the Rockies. Ontario's pulp and paper industry, on the other hand, is controlled by the English.

I arrived in Dubreuilville from Hearst on a slow, winding train that cut through seductively beautiful forest marked by fresh lakes filled with fish, small lumber outposts, Indian settlements, and trappers' camps. Everyone on the train knew one another and a visitor to Dubreuilville was something of an event. "Someone will be meeting you I hope," said the conductor as the train stopped at a small clearing in the forest. There was no sign of a station and no indication of a town.

Dubreuilville looks like any other company town with its identical bungalows and rows of trailers, but unlike other such towns, religion plays a particularly important role in the lives of the residents. On a hill in the centre of town, looking down upon every house, is a church with a fluorescent mauve cross. It was built by Napoléon Dubreuil with the help of the sawmill workers, who were forced to contribute from their pay cheques toward its construction. "I called the church Sainte-Cécile-de-Dubreuilville after my mother," explained Napoléon, who still regards the town as a kind of missionary outpost. "God helped me to make Dubreuilville what it is today."

Now retired, Nap Dubreuil, as the family calls him, still does a little business in a modest room off his apartment in the town's one and only hotel-residence. Although he looks as strong and wily as a peasant, he is filled with a missionary zeal that seems out of keeping with his history as a hard-nosed entrepreneur. His tiny office is as simple as a monk's cell. Religious calendars, pictures of St. Joseph, and a prominent photograph of Mother Teresa, who works with the poor in Calcutta, hang on the walls.

"It was always my dream to set up a real parish," he said as he sat by the window, staring off into the distance. "All our settlements had a church and a school. We were never interested in lumber camps with no women or children. We believed in family life. Making money was not the most important thing. Setting up a real community was our goal," he said, giving me religious cards to take home.

The building of a church was the psychological starting point for each of the three villages the Dubreuils have created in Nouvel-Ontario. In his poem "L'église," Jean-Marc Dalpé writes about the importance of the church for the French parishes in Ontario:

We built our church
put our signature on the land
and signed a contract with the Lord

The church is our pride
set like a precious stone

into the highest hill
for all the men, women, and children
forests, streams, and fields
to marvel at.[2]

Because of these feelings, the Dubreuils found it quite natural to impose a tax on the workers to help pay for the church. In Quebec the Catholic church still has the legal right to demand a tithe from its members, though it abandoned the practice around 1960 at the beginning of the Quiet Revolution. In Dubreuilville a tax for the building of the church continued until the early 1970s. Not everyone in the community supported the idea of a compulsory deduction from their salaries but, according to the old-timers, the workers had no choice. "Anyone who didn't agree with it more or less had to leave," said one worker whose friend left Dubreuilville in a huff over the question in the late 1960s.

The church is still a focal point of the village, but the sawmill is the mainstay of the community. The Dubreuil brothers have made a fortune from the business and the workers make good salaries — $33,000 a year in the forest in 1982, and $22,000 in the sawmill. Yet the town looks as scrubbed and spare as a new colonial settlement. Like the Hutterite villages in western Canada, Dubreuilville takes advantage of the most up-to-date technology but seems to reject the excesses of modern living.

The town has 1,200 people, but there is no bar or *brasserie* where people can unwind over a few drinks after work. The only hotel is a simple, two-story residence with a small restaurant where one can get wine and liquor only with meals. There is no discothèque, no drug store with magazines or a soda fountain, no laundromat: in short, no place to hang out. One general store, which used to be owned and run by the Dubreuils, provides everything. Apart from the sawmill, the church, and the elementary school, activities centre around outdoor sports and hunting. My arrival coincided with the hunting season, and many people were carrying huge moose heads on their cars to enter in Dubreuilville's annual moose contest. Mounted deer heads, bear rugs, and wolf skins are normal home adornments and the freezers are always full of game.

Canadian poetry is filled with references to the brutalities of the frontier, where people wantonly rape and kill nature. This is partly because, in Canada, we see nature as hostile and deceitful. E.J. Pratt evokes this feeling in his poem "Towards the Last Spike":

> Whether alive or dead the bush resisted:
> Alive, it must be slain with axe and saw,
> If dead, it was in tangle at their feet.
> The ice could hit men as it hit the spruces.
> Even the rivers had betraying tricks.

The French in northern Ontario have been as guilty as other Canadians of pillaging nature. French lumber entrepreneurs, for example, helped obliterate the greenery around the Sudbury basin by cutting too many trees thereby causing erosion. But nature sometimes wreaks vengeance, as Hearst novelist Doric Germain knows so well. His adventure story, *La vengeance de l'orignal*, describes how two hunters ignore the rules of hunting and shoot a moose from a low-flying airplane. When they strap the heavy animal to the plane and try to take off for Hearst, the engine breaks down, leaving the pair stranded in the wilderness. Rescued, they later return to pan for gold but stay too late in the season and die in an early winter blizzard. The harsh frontier mentality that Germain describes in this book, a best-seller in the north, can be found in towns such as Hearst.

Dubreuilville, however, is different. There is a softness to the people that comes from their respect for nature and their attachment to simple living. The residents enjoy hunting but, like the Indians, they see themselves as part of the forest, not pitted against it.

This feeling of harmony with nature is one of the themes of Franco-Ontarian literature. Jean-Marc Dalpé expresses this in a poem called "Hommes et femmes d'ici."

> the silence
> and the space
> in your eyes
>
> remind us
> of our ties to the earth
> her changing seasons

Rivers breaking up in spring
Forests full of snow
Fields at harvest-time

remind us
of our ancient ancestral bonds
with the bear and wolf
the hare, the partridge and the swallow

with all that grows, that moves
all that breathes

Our History is written
in your hearts
and smiles.[3]

André Paiement also reflects this attachment to nature in his play *La vie et les temps de Médéric Boileau*. After fifty-four years in the lumber camps, working for the "American Lumber and Export Company of Canada," Boileau is told he is too old to work and dismissed. Until the 1940s, there were no unions in the lumber industry and conditions were tough. Leaving the camp in a state of confusion and dejection, Boileau wends his way through the huge forest of Lac-des-Loups. As darkness falls, he hears the cries of wolves, who slowly move in to form a close circle around him. As Paiement tells it:

He could feel their warm moist breath on his back and, looking up, he saw thick drool dripping from their jaws. Close to madness, Médéric jumped up and, with all the force he could muster, cried out in desperation—evoking the only power that might help—"ALDEGE" [his childhood friend].

The wolves lept back in surprise. He didn't understand why they were afraid, however, without a second's hesitation, he began to howl at the top of his voice. They scattered like wild birds from this creature that could speak their language. Médéric howled louder and louder. The wolves hid in the shelter of the trees and, watching him from a distance like curious rabbits, gave forth several fearful howls. Médéric answered in a similar tone.

He then prowled in a circle, calling to them gently in his wolf voice. Tame as kittens, they came to lie down at their master's side. As the whistling of the wind in the branches changed to a calm breath, Médéric stroked the long fur of his new friends.

"Aldège, I am going to come and visit you. But I think I'll miss the woods. God Almighty! What does the city have that you can't find in the forest?"

And as the fire died down to embers, Médéric drifted off to sleep among the wolves.[4]

Dubreuilville people show the same attachment to their natural surroundings as Médéric Boileau. On Saturdays and Sundays, some people spend the entire day trekking in the woods on skis and snowshoes. In the evening they mount their snowmobiles and disappear into the woods for a *tourtière* supper at the rustic Alouette Club. Others journey further afield along trails blazed by the wood cutters. Gathering around a camp fire deep in the forest, they sing French songs, tell stories, and reminisce about the early days with the Dubreuils. In a town that only started receiving French television in the 1970s, the art of story-telling has not faded, and the Dubreuils are a favourite subject.

Napoléon Dubreuil and his three brothers, Marcel, Augustin, and Joachim, left Taschereau, Quebec, after the Second World War to seek their fortune in Ontario. Their father had a tiny sawmill and store in the town, but after he died the brothers could not get enough wood to keep the operation going. Since there were more wood cutting concessions available in northern Ontario, they migrated across the border with hundreds of other Quebecers.

Napoléon Dubreuil set up a sawmill in Timmins in 1948. Leaving his brothers in charge, he and his wife spent the next winter near Kirkland Lake with a gang of lumberjacks, chopping trees and cutting them at a rented sawmill. Until the 1970s lumber camps in northern Ontario were rough and ready operations cut off from any normal community or family life. In 1949, after a cold and isolated winter cooped up with restless lumberjacks, Napoléon decided to break with this tradition. "When I was in Kirkland Lake I decided two things," he said. "First, I would never set up another lumber camp without wives and children. Second, any community I created would be exclusively French. At Kirkland Lake, French and English lumberjacks fought, and I didn't like it."

The first real community the Dubreuils created was at Mountain Ash Lake, near Chapleau, in 1949, where they secured a three-year government contract to cut wood burnt in a forest fire. All the workers were from Quebec. "It was tough setting things up at Mountain Ash Lake," he recalled. "We moved one sawmill from Timmins and another from Kirkland Lake. We were twelve families then. After we got the sawmills in, we built houses, a church, and a school. After a while we were able to find a priest to come once a month. I remember our first Christmas," he mused with a faraway look in his eyes. "We couldn't get a priest to come, so we did the service ourselves."

There were about twenty-five other sawmill companies with contracts at Mountain Ash Lake, but Napoléon claims he and his brothers were the only ones to make any money. The secret of the Dubreuils' success was that they were leaders of a closely knit commune, rather than fly-by-night operators with an itinerant band of lumberjacks who couldn't be counted on when times got rough. The Dubreuils could depend on the loyalty of their people when they most needed it.

"We were all very close," explained Napoléon. "People stayed with us. They didn't leave. The children of some of the people who worked with us at our later settlement in Magpie are now working with us here in Dubreuilville. When we got into financial difficulties, we could make an agreement with people to delay their pay—often for a whole season. We never wanted to borrow."

When the Mountain Ash Lake contract expired, the Dubreuils moved their tribe to Magpie, at an old mining site on the Magpie River between Wawa and Hawk Junction, some twenty kilometres from the Algoma Central Railway line. The railway company gave them a contract to cut ties and a woods concession to go with it. Through relatives and friends in Taschereau and La Sarre, the group had expanded to include twenty French-Canadian families. The Dubreuils salvaged what they could from Mountain Ash Lake, but once again people had to build homes, school, and church. In 1961 the Dubreuils moved to the present site of Dubreuilville with a larger woods concession on the railway line and a tract of land for a final and more elaborate town.

Until 1975 Dubreuilville operated as the personal preserve of the Dubreuils. The homes, the general store, the residence-hotel, the restaurant—everything except the school and the sports arena—was owned by the family. When people went shopping, they ran up bills which were deducted from their pay cheques. Law and order was enforced by the Dubreuils, who banished employees from the town if they beat their wives, drank too much, or got into fights. The gate at the entrance to the Dubreuilville road thirty kilometres away ensured that only those chosen by the family came in. Attendance at mass was expected. In Dubreuilville the lines dividing church, state, and employer were barely perceptible. Everything revolved around the Dubreuils.

The residents of the town were not like the French in Quebec who revolted against paternalism and supported the rise of militant unions to defend their interests. Quebec was the spiritual home of the people who lived in Dubreuilville, but like most expatriates, they were strangers to events there. For years they were happy living in isolation. The Dubreuils shared this state of mind—their daily lives did not greatly differ from those of the wood cutters and the sawmill workers. All the houses, for example, were exactly the same. The four Dubreuil brothers gave the impression that they were no more affluent than anyone else. They hunted and socialized with their neighbours at the Alouette Club and sent their children to the same school. As the years passed, however, they became very rich.

From the very beginning, the Dubreuils kept up with the latest sawmill technology and regularly introduced new equipment to their constantly expanding plant. In the late 1950s, before they moved to Dubreuilville, they developed a cutting method which allowed them to harvest tree-tops as well. "This was something which everyone considered innovative," said Jean-Paul Dubreuil, son of Napoléon and head of production at the sawmill. "We had people from Sweden and the United States investigating what we were doing. Since we've been in Dubreuilville, we've changed our machinery three times."

Although the town progressed in terms of technology and business, socially it stood still. The family eventually realized it could no longer continue filling the roles of boss, policeman, and mayor: the town was becoming too large and diversified to be run like an extended family where everyone knew his place.

In 1975 the Ontario government sent in Dubreuilville's first police force: the only one-man detachment in the province. Constable Bob Pilon took the job and, apart from an eighteen-month stint in Penetanguishene, he has been there ever since. By the time Pilon arrived, the people of Dubreuilville had developed their own brand of law and order which they handed out to one another in a private and sometimes brutal way, out of sight of the Dubreuils. It took Pilon—who comes from Sudbury and has always worked in Franco-Ontarian communities—a year to bring the town under control. When he left for Penetanguishene, another policeman took his place and the town took a downward turn. On his return, a couple of young delinquents broke into a garage and shot at him. Once he was out of the hospital and back at work, Dubreuilville calmed down and returned to normal.

Another important change took place when Viateur Champagne, a former wood cutter and militant CNTU unionist from the Gaspé, blew into town looking for work. Champagne had no intentions of organizing a union when he arrived in Dubreuilville in 1975. "I'd never even heard of the town when I was in Quebec," he said. "When I left, I was en route to Vancouver. I'd been burning the candle at both ends, spending enormous amounts of money drinking and carousing. One day a friend of mine and I decided to drop everything—job, wife, and family—to go west. Our money lasted until we arrived in Hearst. We stayed there a while and then went to Wawa, where we heard there were jobs in Dubreuilville."

By 1975 the Dubreuilville workers had organized a rather tame employees association which the company preferred to the Lumber and Sawmill Workers' Union active in the other northern Ontario sawmills. For about a year, Champagne took a back seat at meetings and stayed silent. He wanted to bask in the otherworldly ambiance of this little French town he had discovered in the middle of nowhere. After a while, his fellow workers began pressing him for his views. Impressed with his experience, they elected him vice-president of their association. In no time it started behaving like a real union. Champagne took charge of negotiations with the family. "We went to the Dubreuils and asked them for the same conditions as the other unionized sawmill workers, and we told them we'd strike if we didn't get them," he said.

The Dubreuils couldn't believe they would ever see the day when their loyal band of workers, some of whom had weathered years with them in Mountain Ash Lake and Magpie, would join a picket line. But in 1978, when they refused to give the union what it wanted, the workers followed Champagne's advice and went on strike. "It was unnerving" he said, "because as the only experienced unionist, I was responsible for everything." After ten days the Dubreuils gave in. A month later, in a union election, the workers elected Champagne president, a post he has held ever since. "We've done well since then," he said. "In our last contract, we went beyond what the unions in the other sawmills have been able to get."

Champagne still sees himself as a Quebecer, but he loves living in Dubreuilville. "The town has a strange fascination for me. It's a simple place where people work, enjoy the outdoors, and spend time with their families. Frankly, it saved me. I found calm and serenity here. Shortly after I arrived I brought my wife and children here and changed my way of life," he said.

Champagne intends to stay in the town, even though he finds certain social attitudes foreign. "In Dubreuilville people are not politicized the way we are in Quebec. Culturally they're like Quebecers, but politically they're something else. They've been very cut off. Radio-Canada came here only a few years ago, so they're not used to following political events with any regularity. All the developments that took place in the Quebec union movement have passed them by. Union education has been totally lacking. When I arrived, salaries and conditions were way below those of sawmill workers elsewhere. People didn't know what to do— they were dissatisfied, but they were afraid to stand up to the Dubreuils. Over the past few years, that has changed. Now they are much more aggressive, but relations with the company are good."

The strengthening of the union and its effect on relations between the Dubreuils and their workers has been matched by important shifts in the internal workings of the company. It, too, has been forced to modernize. Some executive positions are now going to people outside the Dubreuil family. "Times are changing," Napoléon observed with a certain nostalgia. "Different qualifications are now required for a successful business. Everything is more complicated than it was when I started out. To compete, we must stay abreast of technological and financial developments." The four Dubreuil brothers who built the town made their fortunes through hard work and determination, but not enough of the younger Dubreuils are seeking the necessary administrative and technical qualifications to run the business. As top posts go to outsiders, the family's grip of Dubreuilville will weaken.

The coming of municipal government in 1977 also changed the atmosphere of the town. The road to the highway, for example, became a public road, so the Dubreuils could no longer close it off. The old gate is still there, but it is no more than a relic of the past. Democracy in municipal government, however, does not yet exist in Dubreuilville. The board of trustees which runs the town is appointed by the Ontario government, not elected by the people. Called an Improvement District rather than a municipality, Dubreuilville must submit its minutes to the Sudbury region of the Ontario municipal affairs department.

The Dubreuil brothers are only one of a dozen francophone families who have established lumber firms in northern Ontario. The others live in towns such as Timmins, Hearst, Chapleau, Kirkland Lake, and Cochrane. Unmistakably French, the lumber barons braved it out on the frontier, where life was hard and perseverance paid off. As they established themselves, they learned English, figured out how to cope with the Ontario authorities, and waded into profitable American markets and financial circles.

The lumber barons of Nouvel-Ontario are no more worried about cultural survival or assimilation than the miners of Sudbury. Both groups have forged a place for themselves in Ontario. Though part of the beleaguered French minority, as individuals they do not feel diminished or victimized.

Living in French is important to the Franco-Ontarian lumber entrepreneurs, but carving out a portion of the Ontario economy has been even more so. This has entailed operating with efficiency in both French and English. The lumbermen are not as bicultural as Franco-Ontarian financiers Robert Campeau or Paul Desmarais, but they do not find living in two cultures threatening. Economic success has been their principal goal and, to reach it, they have functioned as individuals. The lumber and sawmill industry was one they could build up from scratch, starting as lumberjacks.

For twenty years, from 1960 to 1980, the French lumber entrepreneurs profited from exciting boom years. Now they are worried about the economics of the wood industry, which was hit hard in 1981 by a slump in the North American construction industry. What concerns the lumber barons over the long term, however, is the availability of wood for future expansion.

Jean-Paul Dubreuil is head of a special committee composed of sixteen independent sawmill entrepreneurs, formed under the Ontario Lumber Manufacturers Association. This committee is pushing the Ontario government to reallocate wood concessions so the sawmills will be able to expand. In Quebec and New Brunswick, pulp and paper companies must give up their surplus wood to the sawmill firms. In spite of continuous pressure, this system has not been adopted in Ontario. Jean-Paul Dubreuil is aware that this will not completely solve the problem. "It's a very difficult situation," he said. "We are hoping for changes in the wood allocation, but even with that, some of the present sawmill companies may face difficulties. Amalgamations may be necessary."

Changes may be in store for the lumber barons, but their exploits as pioneers are still the stuff of legends in Nouvel-Ontario. In the mid-1970s the members of the Théâtre de Nouvel-Ontario in Sudbury were so fascinated by the story of the Dubreuils and their fiefdom in the woods that they wrote a rock opera about it called *Lavalléville*, which toured Nouvel-Ontario. Other Franco-Ontarian plays such as *La vie et les temps de Médéric Boileau* explore the nomadic lives of lumberjacks.

The busy mining town of Timmins, with its shacks abandoned from earlier gold mining days, harbours as many exciting stories of the past as Dubreuilville. The presiding lumber baron of Timmins is Gaston Malette, a small, shy man who still has trouble with English. Despite appearances, he is the Horatio Alger hero of Nouvel-Ontario with the biggest lumber operation. Originally from Taschereau, Quebec, Malette first worked for the Dubreuils in Quebec and Ontario. While still in his twenties, he bought a sawmill in Timmins from them and went into business with his brothers. He now has many plants in northern Ontario and is expanding into Quebec.

Most of the French lumber barons keep to Ontario, but Malette insists on working in Quebec as well. Speaking on his behalf, Timmins' broadcast millionaire Conrad Lavigne, who is on the board of directors of one of Malette's firms, explained the expansion of the company into Quebec this way: "If the province separates, we don't want to be treated as though we're English from Ontario," he joked. "But seriously, we have Quebec business and we want to keep it. Besides we're nearer American and overseas markets in Quebec."

There are sentimental reasons, too, for Malette's desire to be in Quebec. Malette has done well in Ontario, but when he needed money at a crucial point in his career to expand his lumber business, he was forced to go to Montreal. I met Malette at a press conference in Timmins where the treasurer of Ontario, Frank Miller, announced—in French—that the Ontario government would be lending Malette $1.5 million to enlarge his particle board plant. Ontario's financial institutions were not always so forthcoming: in 1972, when Malette needed a large loan to launch his wafer board plant, the Toronto banks turned their backs on him.

"The reasons for this were simple," he explained without rancour. "We were French and we were not engineers. The Toronto banks felt we didn't have the necessary education." Malette dropped out of school at age fourteen and later attended a Montreal business college, but he had had twenty successful years in the lumbering business when he asked for his loan. "I went to the Banque Nationale in Montreal when the Toronto banks shut the door. It was the first financial institution to give me a big loan. After that," he smiled, "I didn't have any further problems with Toronto."

The biggest concentration of French lumber entrepreneurs is in Hearst—the moose capital of Canada—at the junction of the Algoma Central and Canadian National Railways. A huge statue of a bull moose towering over a tiny tourist bureau at the entrance to the town underlines the attraction of Hearst as a hunting and fishing paradise. The real business of the town, however, is wood. Fuel depots, lumber warehouses, railway sidings, and sales outlets for trucks crowd the highway on the edge of town. From early morning to late at night, trucks loaded with wood rumble through the community. To accommodate the new business which keeps Hearst humming, garish motels advertising sauna baths and swimming pools keep popping up.

Hearst is a growing town of 6,000 with a predominantly French population. Because of the activities of four key families—the Fontaines, Lecours, Lévesques, and Gosselins—all the economic and political power of the town is French. Ironically, Hearst started off as a railway depot employing anglophones around the turn of the century. The soil and climate also permitted subsistence farming. By 1920, however, wood had become the town's principal industry, and farmers and lumberjacks from Abitibi and Lac-Saint-Jean had started moving in. When the Americans lost their concessions to cut wood in the forties and fifties, the French filled the vacuum. By 1960 Hearst was more French than English. Today there are not enough English students to justify a full English high school program, a source of resentment for some English families who feel they must send their children elsewhere once they finish elementary school.

Lumber and related industries keep the town moving ahead at a fast pace. "Hearst is developing like no other community in the north," said Jacques Côté, Hearst's municipal administrator. "There are about 500 entrepreneurs connected with the wood industry here. Until the economic slump of 1981 and 1982, buildings were going up everywhere. In 1980, for example, the town had $5 million worth of building contracts."

Prices dropped dramatically in the wood industry in 1981, but until then, money was coming in so quickly that people didn't know what to do with it. Most of the sawmill owners are people with simple tastes, but they have bought private planes, remote chalets in prime hunting territory, and even Florida condominiums. "Under normal circumstances, money really rolls in this town," noted an official at the Canadian Imperial Bank of Commerce: he estimated the number of millionaires in Hearst to be around twenty-five.

Hearst's well-to-do, however, still look like hearty lumberjacks fresh from the camps. No one in town seems to own a suit: garb at the sawmill offices is work boots, jeans, and, in winter, bulky leather jackets. Although Hearst has an active family life, it is essentially a man's town. Hotels and restaurants at night are filled with lumbermen swilling beer and telling stories after a hard day's trek to the woods. Drinking, in fact, is such a problem that the ranks of Alcoholics Anonymous are swelling.

On my first night in Hearst, I combed the town for a restaurant with a woman in it, but only one had mixed clientele. When I asked where I could go later in the evening, the waitress suggested half-seriously that I drop in on the Alcoholics Anonymous congress at the high school. Ten minutes later, I was sitting with AA members from towns across Nouvel-Ontario at their annual weekend get-together. People from Hearst, Kapuskasing, Iroquois Falls, Mattice, Timmins, Kirkland Lake, and Cochrane—all of them French—packed the school auditorium.

"*Mon nom est André,*" said a man in a solemn voice at the opening of the congress, "*et je suis alcoholique.*" Standing at a lectern on the stage, André talked about his nightmarish life before he stopped drinking. Except for the references to the sawmills and the Ontario north, the meeting could have been anywhere in Quebec. Like most activities in Hearst, everything took place in French. At the beginning of the congress, there was a token welcome in English for the handful of anglophones present, but after some brief exchanges they were ushered into separate quarters.

Hearst may be a rough frontier town with its share of social problems, but the new riches of the community give the town a sophisticated look. Over the past few years, hundreds of sprawling homes, many with swimming pools, have sprung up. For the size of the community, services are more than ample: a hospital, old people's homes, an Olympic-size pool, arena, curling rink, golf course, and airport. Hearst College, which is affiliated with Laurentian University, offers a full B.A. program in French. Originally a *collège classique*, and now a secular institution, the college adds a noticeable intellectual and cultural dimension to the town.

"Every second week," said French writer and professor Doric Germain, "we have some cultural activity at the college—a play, a *chansonnier*, a poetry reading." Though small, the college has produced poets, playwrights, and novelists over the years. Germain, who was born in Hearst, is the author of two published novels, both of them about trappers.

One of the most important persons in town is undoubtedly René Fontaine, who was mayor of Hearst for fourteen years until 1981. Fontaine's grandfather Noé built one of the first sawmills in Hearst in the 1940s. By the time he died, he had operations scattered across several towns in Nouvel-Ontario. In the mid-1960s Fontaine's father Zacharie consolidated them in Hearst. Now a partner in United Sawmills, an amalgamation of three different companies, René Fontaine divides his time between work and community activities. By encouraging his fellow sawmill owners to invest heavily in community projects such as the recreation centre, he has helped make Hearst the thriving town that it is.

Fontaine wears woodsmen's clothes wherever he goes. When I first met him, he was dashing into his mayor's office at city hall, sporting work boots, jeans, and a burgundy-coloured leather jacket. He quickly signed some documents then raced off to coach the Lumberkings Midget Hockey team. "I enjoy the kids," he said. "I make a point of finding time for them."

A third generation Franco-Ontarian, Fontaine is proud of his heritage and wants French culture in the north to thrive. When he was mayor, he pushed to give French more status in the town. Because Hearst is in Ontario and English is the language of business in the outside world, French often gets short shrift. "The town is 85 per cent French, and about a third of the population speaks no English," said Fontaine. "Yet until 1978, all the minutes of municipal council meetings were in English only. I wanted the council to recognize both languages in its work." As a result of Fontaine's efforts, the municipality of Hearst is now officially bilingual: both languages are used in minutes, by-laws, documents, and council meetings.

The three other French lumber families in Hearst—the Lévesques, Lecours, and Gosselins—are almost as deeply rooted in Franco-Ontario as the Fontaines. They are all second-generation Franco-Ontarian families whose fathers or uncles started sawmills that sons and nephews eventually took over and expanded. The Lévesques now have two independent companies run by different wings of the family.

Yvon Lévesque runs the town's largest sawmill operation. A strong, broad-shouldered man, he branched off from his father and brother at the age of twenty-seven to build his own plywood and particle board plants. Like Gaston Malette, he had trouble finding money. "No one in either Quebec or Ontario would look at me," he said. "I had no track record. But I had no intentions of giving up, so I went to New York and found the money there. In 1969, when I built my particle board plant, I went to Germany and Belgium for financing."

The years 1981 and 1982 were particularly difficult for the lumber entrepreneurs because of the drastic slump in the construction industry in the United States and Canada. After years of rising profits, prices suddenly dropped out of the lumber market. At one pont in 1982, 40 per cent of the work force in Hearst was unemployed. To fight their unexpected economic and social problems, people in the town banded together like an extended family. The *caisse populaire* formed a special credit committee to ensure that families did not lose their homes. Day-time recreation programs for the unemployed were created by the municipality. At one point mayor Gilles Gagnon, sawmill owner René Fontaine, and municipal administrator Jacques Côté conducted special sessions at the high school to explain the crisis to the students. "Many young people are used to Florida vacations and fancy Christmases," explained Côté. "The students had to know what was going on."

Even in normal times, Hearst tends to function like a traditional village where people take care of one another. The sawmill owners in Hearst are in competition, but they also see themselves as members of a select club who must co-operate. In the late 1960s, when business was highly profitable, they formed the Claybelt Lumber Company to handle some domestic and foreign sales. The firm is run by Paul Zorzetto, a warm and expansive former lumberjack who is also mayor of the small French town of Mattice, near Hearst.

Zorzetto's office, located on the outskirts of Hearst, looks more like a bookie's den than a sales office for five, multi-million-dollar lumber companies. Cigar smoke clouds the office. Scraps of paper with numbers scratched on them are scattered everywhere. The day I dropped in, a couple of dubious-looking fellows with day-old beards were slouched on a broken-down couch, reading papers. At a desk piled with an unruly mass of papers sat Zorzetto, a phone glued to each ear, barking out figures and negotiating deals. With a thick cigar stuffed in his mouth and a tight, canary-yellow T-shirt cutting into his bulging arms, Zorzetto looked more like a character out of a comic strip than a high-powered lumber salesman.

"We started this outfit," he said between calls, "because we didn't trust the Toronto wholesalers. They seemed to be offering low prices, so we decided we'd be better off doing our own transactions. About 20 per cent of all the Hearst sawmill sales go through this office." In the tradition of the lumber kings, Zorzetto learned about the business from the bottom up. Originally from France, he came to Hearst in 1955 to work as a lumberjack. Later he became a paymaster in lumber camps. Eventually he moved into administrative work and selling.

Like René Fontaine, Zorzetto believes Franco-Ontarian culture can survive. "In Mattice, we are 1,200 people—and we are completely French. All the municipal business of the town is done in French. In fact, we are unilingual. Quite a feat in Ontario!" he grinned. But in spite of the fact that the Hearst area is mainly French, Zorzetto says that people are very conscious of living in an English province. "People here are practical. These are French towns around here, but "*la piastre* ... the buck*," he cried, jabbing the air, "*c'est en anglais!*"

Chapter 9

How long would it take a French Canadian to rise to the top of Sun Life? Pretty damn long ... Ownership is the key to power. French Canadians have not been able to think of the long-term in business because they've had no economic power. That is what must change.

Paul Desmarais

Professional managers work to advance their careers and to acquire power. They don't have ownership to protect that power, so they behave like a union when their interests are threatened. That was what I was up against.

Robert Campeau

Tycoons from Sudbury

August 27, 1980, is a day that Sudbury-born entrepreneur Robert Campeau will never forget. It all began with a trip to the summer retreat of Kenneth White, then chairman and president of the English establishment's most venerable financial institution, Royal Trustco. In thirty years, Robert Campeau had transformed himself from an Inco labourer with a pick and shovel into the boy wonder of Canadian developers, with assets of over a billion dollars. Poised for yet another quantum leap up the scale of power and respectability, he was bent on negotiating one of the biggest corporate take-overs in Canadian history.

Robert Campeau and Kenneth White represent totally different, and competing, approaches to business in Canada. Campeau is a self-made man from a poor French-Canadian family, who started with nothing more than a grade-eight education and the will to become a powerful entrepreneur. Unorthodox and aggressive, he stands for the spirit of free enterprise in Canadian business. White is a corporate bureaucrat whose authority flows from his virtual custody of Royal Trustco. Conservative and cautious—his eye ever on the English tradition—he owes his power not to personal ownership of millions of Royal Trust dollars, but to his ability to inspire confidence among an inner circle in the top Canadian corporations and brokerage houses.

For years White had been part of the English establishment in Montreal. Like many of his friends and colleagues, he moved to Toronto when head offices fled Quebec in the wake of restrictive provincial language legislation. The official reason Royal Trustco executives gave for their shift to Toronto between 1976 and 1978 was their need to be closer to other head offices: power was moving west and the company was following. Quebec nationalism and the rise of the Parti Québécois were not factors, they claimed.

Even though they were Montrealers with roots in Quebec, White and other anglophone business leaders seemed only too eager to pack up and leave. They belonged to a community that was confused about the turn of events in Quebec, and that harboured bitter feelings toward French Quebecers for depriving them of their 200-year-old tradition of hegemony in business. Many business leaders would not admit it, but they allowed personal feelings of incomprehension and rage at social change in Quebec to influence the course of the companies they directed.

Campeau was oblivious of all this as he stepped through the door of White's summer home in Bromont, seventy kilometres from Montreal in the Eastern Townships. He was like an Olympic runner who can already feel a gold medal in the palm of his hand. Campeau's origins were more humble than those of White, but he exuded as much class and breeding. Tall and slight, with a graceful walk and a ruddy Scottish complexion inherited from his mother, he looked like a Kenneth Galbraith about to drop a puzzling economic idea on an unwitting audience.

His mission to Bromont was respectful of the protocol expected in such situations. On the surface it was perfectly simple: he had come to inform White that he would be making a $413 million bid for control of Royal Trustco. Backed by Greenshields stockbrokers in Montreal and the Bank of Nova Scotia in Toronto, he would pay shareholders willing to tender their stock $21 rather than the $16 current market price if he secured 50 per cent of the total shares.

When White saw Campeau roll into his driveway, he rushed out of his house and greeted him with open arms, thinking he had come to negotiate a big mortgage for one of his properties. He was shocked when he found out the real purpose of Campeau's visit. As president of Royal Trustco, White carried enormous influence in the Canadian business community; nevertheless, he was subject to the decisions of his board of directors. He could not act alone. Where stock is widely dispersed among many stockholders, as it is at Royal Trustco, the board of directors is the creature of professional managers such as White. When a single shareholder gains control of more than half the stock, the professionals can find themselves in a vulnerable position. If Campeau succeeded in his bid, he would be able to choose the senior executives and plot the course of the company's investments. In other words: a French Canadian from Sudbury, rather than a consortium of the traditional English elite from Montreal, would have the last word on Royal Trustco, not to mention the job held by Kenneth White.

What Campeau was setting out to do was not unusual. Other trust companies in Canada are controlled by individual shareholders. Campeau had made his mark in one field and was expanding into another. A veteran stockbroker in English Montreal who was close to both sides of the Royal Trustco affair described the situation this way: "Campeau was looking for respectability and he deserved it. Sure, he would have streamlined the management, but the Royal Trustco administration needed it."

White had escaped the widening influence of *la francophonie* in Quebec by moving to Ontario, but now, ironically, French power had popped up in an unexpected form in Toronto. Together with Sun Life and the Bank of Montreal, Royal Trustco was old English turf dating back to nineteenth-century Montreal. Those in the inner sanctum of these organizations were jealous of their control.

Campeau had created an impressive empire, but he took risks that old money would never take and functioned by rules that few in the English establishment could accept. He was a member of what Peter Newman has dramatically termed "the brazen new posse of acquisitors [that is] barging into some of the establishment's most prestigious command posts ... and shattering the common ethos that only a short while ago united Canada's commercial elite."[1]

To people in the financial world, Campeau was a mystery. James Lorimer, in his book *The Developers*, attests to this when he says that Campeau runs a "dynamic one-man show, a fact which caused a firm of investment analysts writing about the company in 1972 to confess: 'We are completely bewildered as to how operating control of this type of situation is effectively maintained.'" Lorimer adds that "in spite of outsiders' bewilderment, Campeau has steered his company from success to success" and has "single-handedly built one of the country's largest development corporations."[2] Campeau was obviously an accomplished businessman, but to White and other managers his takeover bid was nothing less than a challenge to the old order.

After Campeau revealed his plan, White dispensed with pleasantries and flew into a rage. "I don't like you or Conrad Black or the Bronfmans," he told a startled Campeau during the meeting at his country home, "people who think they can just go ahead and make an offer for a company." The bid, White declared, will "damage English / French relations in Canada ... You may think that money talks ... but there's not going to be any white knight."

White was not prepared to submit to new French-Canadian money from Sudbury, even if it spoke English and supported Canadian unity. Before escorting his shaken guest from his home, White had a word of warning: "I will call my friends and lock up 51 percent of the stock before you can turn around. I have got ways to persuade friends of mine to go along with me, and I will." White then dismissed Campeau and walked away, then he turned back and said: "I am getting on the phone now, getting all my team together, and we are going to stop you."[3]

White immediately started calling people in English financial circles to help him fight Campeau. The next day he recruited McLeod Young Weir investment dealers in Toronto to line up all the friendly corporations they could think of to undermine the bid. By the end of the manoeuvre, the list of people who rallied behind Royal Trustco looked like a who's who of the English financial elite. The key players were Sun Life, the Bank of Montreal, Toronto-Dominion Bank, Noranda Mines, Commercial Union Assurance, the Oxford Development Group, and Olympia and York. But many other important institutions and individuals also played a part. Even McGill University became involved. The university could not remain neutral because of the large block of stock it held in its investment portfolio. Along with certain institutes and colleges affiliated to the university, it refused to tender its Royal Trustco shares. The chancellor of McGill, Conrad Harrington, had been a Royal Trustco president, so he could be counted upon to support the current management. White left no stones unturned in his attempt to defeat Campeau. According to Montreal investment analysts who followed the affair, even unwitting widows of old monied families received calls from the friends of Royal Trustco. Those with substantial amounts of shares were asked to bypass Campeau's offer and yield their holdings to Royal Trustco sympathizers.

Before Campeau's offer expired five weeks later on October 2, 1980, over 60 per cent of Royal Trustco shares changed hands on the stock market at prices below his bid. In a few weeks, the friends of Royal Trustco took control. Before the battle was over, however, the Ontario Securities Commission had stepped in to investigate possible violations of security laws. If companies act together to buy more than 20 per cent of a firm without saying so publicly, they are violating federal corporation regulations as well as Ontario and Quebec security laws. In January 1981, at public hearings, the Ontario Securities Commission established that White had induced friends of Royal Trustco to make a competing takeover bid for the institution without necessary disclosure. Collusion had taken place but there was no way to undo the damage. White and John Scholes, who took over as president of Royal Trustco in April 1982, were personally slapped on the wrists and prevented from trading on the stock exchange for a short period of time, but Royal Trustco itself was not affected. Eventually, Campeau sold what Royal Trustco stock he had and withdrew quietly from the scene.

Early in 1982, however, the federal Department of Consumer and Commercial Affairs filed a suit against Royal Trustco on behalf of the small shareholders who lost money as a result of the company's action in fending off Campeau's takeover bid. The list of Royal Trustco directors named in the suit contains some of the most prominent names in Canadian business, including Alistair Campbell, former chairman of Sun Life Assurance Company of Canada; Conrad Harrington, former chairman of Royal Trustco and chancellor of McGill University, and Angus MacNaughton, chairman of Genstar Corporation of Vancouver.

There is no way one can enter the Outaouais region and not be aware of the prodigious activity of Robert Campeau. In Ottawa there is the towering Place de Ville office complex. Across the river in Hull there is the impressive brick and glass Les Terrasses de la Chaudière. Scattered throughout the region are the thousands of homes that secured Campeau's future as a developer.

One of the most prestigious hotels built by Campeau is the Auberge de la Chaudière in Hull. On a sunny day in June 1981, six months after the Royal Trustco affair had faded from the news, Campeau was finishing up an elegant luncheon meeting with a group of francophone businessmen. A series of phone calls interrupted the meal as he talked in French and English with cabinet ministers, company presidents, and his own senior executives. Campeau is one of the few successful Canadian businessmen outside Quebec to run a large-scale bilingual company. Like Paul Desmarais, who also comes from Sudbury, he operates with ease in both English and French milieus.

Campeau was not always so polished and self-assured. A francophone from the rough and tumble frontier city of Sudbury, he grew up in the thirties when life was tough. His father was a mechanic with his own garage, but he lost it during the Depression. One of seven children, Campeau was known in his neighbourhood as a scrappy kid who knew how to defend his turf.

"French people in Sudbury had a fight for two things," he recalled after his luncheon guests had left. "One was to preserve our French culture and traditions. The other was to get ahead in the world. In Sudbury, life was easier for Finns and Ukrainians who were prepared to assimilate. Everyone resented us because we wouldn't give up our language. That was why we had more trouble getting ahead in the mines and other places."

Campeau first experienced this resentment as a boy while selling newspapers on the street. "I had to fight like mad to get a good corner. It taught me that I had to assert myself if I wanted to get anywhere." Like many francophone children of his generation, Campeau quit school at the end of elementary school. There were no French public high schools in Ontario at the time, and with seven young mouths to feed in the Campeau family, the Collège du Sacré-Coeur was too expensive, so he went out to work.

Campeau's first job was at Inco cleaning up after machinists. Determined to move up in a hurry, he stayed on almost every day for a second shift to learn the trade. In a year, he was calling himself an expert machinist and moving from one plant to another in various Ontario towns, learning new skills. By the age of twenty-four he was a foreman at International Paper in Hull.

At this point, Campeau decided to become an entrepreneur. Married with one child, he wanted a home for his family and a trial run as a contractor. He had watched housing contractors at work and was sure he could do better. "Even the bad contractors made good money," he said. "I figured I could make a fortune." His first home cost $5,000 and he sold it immediately for $7,300. A year later he had forty homes under construction. Four years later, at the age of twenty-nine his construction company's assets were already half a million dollars. In twenty years they multiplied to more than half a billion.

In 1966 Campeau took his first major step beyond suburban housing when he built the Place de Ville project in Ottawa, where the federal government rents office space. Now he has luxury hotels, race tracks, shopping centres, office towers, and residential properties from Quebec to California. The assets of Campeau Corporation are around $1 billion and his personal fortune is estimated to be worth more than $20 million.

Tough and stubborn, but capable of real generosity, Campeau elicits strong emotions from those who have had any dealings with him. Architects find him somewhat single-minded to work with, but praise his dynamism and guts. "He's willing to take a gamble," said one man who worked with him on a big project. "It's beautiful watching him fly." A tradesman who worked on the Harbour Castle project in Toronto had this to say: "One day he called us all together and gave us a big speech about how he had worked with his hands and knew what it was like and we all had to pull together. I didn't like it much: I would have preferred if he hadn't said anything. It sounded as if we weren't pulling our weight. But you've got to give him credit. At the end of the job, he gave us all a huge banquet; half the crew on Saturday, the other half on Sunday—all we wanted to eat and drink."[4]

Campeau became a construction czar in a very short period of time, but his climb to wealth and power was not without obstacles. During the 1950s his major foe in Ottawa was the legendary Mayor Charlotte Whitton, who did not move quickly enough for Campeau on his building projects. In the early 1970s he ran into financial problems. He had allowed Paul Desmarais to buy controlling interest in his company in the late 1960s; when he decided to buy back control, he borrowed Swiss francs and subsequently lost several million dollars when the dollar fell.

153

Campeau faced his biggest hurdle when he tried to negotiate his way into Royal Trustco, the heart of the English business establishment. However, over the years, he succeeded in penetrating another influential elite—the federal Liberal establishment. Critics of Campeau feel his ties are so close to the federal government that he receives privileged treatment from them on contracts and rental rates. In 1978 Conservative MPs in the House of Commons complained that political connections helped Campeau obtain a lease-purchase agreement which enabled him to build the Terrasses de la Chaudière project in Hull. Later, a Senate committee reported that the rents the federal government was paying in the office complex were above the market rates. Campeau is now the single largest landlord of office space rented by the federal authorities in Ottawa and Hull, a fact which led him to be dubbed the government's "developer by appointment."

Campeau's French origins may have helped him in Ottawa, but they played against him when he tried to take over Royal Trustco, and this hurt him deeply. "Kenneth White just doesn't like French people," he said. "If my name had been MacDonald, it would have been a completely different story. What happened was that the remnants of the Westmount[5] business establishment, who are now in Toronto, and are feeling pretty sore about French people, organized to keep me out."

As he talked about "the Westmount group" his bitterness became more and more apparent. "With their attitudes of exclusiveness, they provoked the radical behaviour we now see in the Parti Québécois." Campeau is a strongly committed federalist who believes in equality of English and French. Prime Minister Trudeau, he believes, has done much to rectify imbalances between the two groups. Campeau is opposed to the Parti Québécois because he feels it encourages inward-looking behaviour, but he blames the English economic elite in Montreal for what he considers the excesses of the government's nationalist policies.

English / French rivalries, as well as those between old and new money, played a role in the defeat of Campeau's takeover bid. Other factors, however, were also involved. According to Campeau, the real issue was a fundamental conflict between professional managers and owner-managers. "Professional managers work to advance their careers and to acquire power. They don't have ownership to protect that power, so they behave like a union when their interests are threatened. That," he said with emphasis, "was what I was up against." The professional managers in corporations, banks, and trust companies work together for stock purchases, loans, and so on, he explained. When White called for help, he could count upon his counterparts in other institutions to give him a hand. Campeau is still smarting from his Royal Trustco experience, but he feels the Westmount group in Canadian business is becoming obsolete and that their role in preventing the bid was their last gasp.

Observers in the investment world say that Greenshields' involvement in the Campeau bid is indicative of a shift in power away from the old English-Protestant elite. Greenshields, a Montreal-based investment firm, is considered to be part of the English establishment; but it does not allow the old school tie to influence its business judgments and recognizes the importance of a rising group of ambitious new entrepreneurs of French and immigrant background. In supporting Campeau, Greenshields wanted to make it clear to all comers—whether from Quebec, Ontario, or the West—that they were not tied to traditional English interests.

Interestingly, Greenshields also handled Paul Desmarais's controversial bid to take over Argus Corporation in 1975. The huge Toronto-based conglomerate was controlled by its president, John "Bud" McDougald, considered to be a pillar of the old English establishment. At the time, McDougald instructed all the companies he controlled to cease dealing with Greenshields, thereby punishing the firm for supporting someone outside the fold. Royal Trustco took similar actions when it stopped all business with the brokerage house, but its decision was only temporary. Greenshields worked on behalf of Desmarais and Campeau because it felt they were solid entrepreneurs. Most developers suffer from persistent litigation but, as Greenshields has pointed out, this was not the case with Campeau.

The Royal Trustco episode reflects the attitudes of exclusiveness characteristic of the English and French communities in Canada. As Ronald Sutherland points out so aptly in *Second Image*,[6] the ethnocentric ideologies of the English and French are a peculiarly Canadian affliction. Campeau suffered at the hands of English exclusivism, but he has been able to rise above his own personal feelings about the affair. In his view, the unhealthy state of English / French relations that has plagued Quebec and Ontario for the past two centuries will eventually disappear.

"We must enter a period of rebuilding and forget about old hostilities," he said. "The last political battle in Ontario will be to make French an official language, and I am convinced that eventually this will happen. A new group of bilingual, bicultural people in central Canada will break down the polarization between French and English."

The beginnings of this trend have already been noticed by people in Quebec such as Liberal MNA Daniel Johnson, son of Quebec's late Union Nationale premier Daniel Johnson. Until his election in 1981 Johnson was a senior executive with Desmarais's Power Corporation. He says English and French students in business administration started meeting and exchanging views during the sixties and seventies in graduate schools across the country. "These people are starting to do business with one another. Westerners are coming east to look for places to put their money, and Quebecers are going west with their services. There's a new interface between French and English that is building up among a new generation of business people in their thirties. Better French / English relations will come first in business; later, we will see its effects in federal and provincial politics."

The man who has done as much as anyone to bring together the two solitudes in Canadian business is Paul Desmarais. Born in Sudbury, he operates out of Montreal, but ranges across Canada, the United States, and Europe. By winning an enviable place for himself in the ranks of Canadian business, Desmarais has widened the field occupied by francophone entrepreneurs.

A member of the newest layer of the Canadian commercial elite, Desmarais won his spurs by manoeuvring, taking risks, and developing a sixth sense about where the most interesting situations were likely to unfold. Like his colleague from Sudbury, Desmarais is very different from representatives of the traditional English establishment with their tight-lipped demeanour and joyless attitude to work. Both Campeau and Desmarais look upon money-making as a great game and engage in lavish life-styles to go with it.

Desmarais's home in Westmount is filled with priceless art treasures and looks like a cross between a small French chateau and a museum. His offices, which are lodged unobtrusively on the seventh floor of the Canada Steamship Building in Montreal, also ring of wealth and refinement. The furniture is antique and the walls are covered with a vast collection of Canadian art: a lush painting by Marc-Aurèle Fortin, others by Riopelle, Varley, Roberts, Jackson, Gagnon, and Lemieux—each displayed with taste and care.

An expert on Napoleon Bonaparte, Desmarais is in many ways himself a driven man who cannot stop looking for new ways to expand his power base. Desmarais's way of coming to decisions and carrying out plans resembles that of a chess grandmaster. Between moves, he vacations in his various mansions, imbibes the best of wines, prowls around art galleries, and gives gala dinners. When his son Paul got married, he threw a party fit for a prince. A New York interior designer flew in to decorate the reception marquee with white baby orchids, and contralto Maureen Forrester sang. Guests included Pierre Trudeau and Jean Chrétien, as well as friends from Europe and the United States, all of whom received airline tickets and weekend accommodation in Montreal with their invitations. Until recently, Desmarais was not able to penetrate the inner sanctum of the old Westmount establishment crowned by Royal Trust and the Bank of Montreal: his friends have always come from the next level down. His cronies, however, have never been exclusively Canadian. Desmarais is part of an international business network and his friends include British newspaper magnates, American industrialists, Arab sheiks, and Swiss bankers.

Desmarais started his climb to financial power in Sudbury in 1951, when he took over his grandfather's bankrupt bus company at the age of twenty-four. The family had intended to sell the company, but Desmarais, who was then studying law at Osgoode Hall in Toronto, persuaded his father to let him try putting the firm back on its feet over a summer. Desmarais became so bitten by the entrepreneurial bug that he never went back to school. In five years, he pulled the company out of a deficit of $384,000 to make a profit of $100,000. A sharp financial nose, dogged determination, and the sheer delight of making a sick company healthy lay behind his first success in the entrepreneurial world and became characteristic of his style and pattern for later manoeuvres.

At the start of his bus company venture, Desmarais was in such financial straits that he was borrowing $3,000 a week for the payroll from the local priest, relatives, various friends—anyone, in fact, who would help him out. Then the Royal Bank cut his line of credit. One day he walked in the Sudbury branch and the bank manager said: "We've got enough of your cheques flying all over the place. We're not going to cash any more of your cheques, do you understand?" Desmarais didn't have any choice, so he said: "Well, to hell with you," and walked out.

Desmarais's bus company had the franchise to carry miners to and from the Inco mine in Copper Cliff. As long as the service continued, he had a chance to work out a solution with Inco. Desperate, he called up the vice-president of Inco, Les Beattie, at his summer camp on Ramsay Lake. Beattie's wife answered the phone just as Beattie was stepping into his car to catch a train for Toronto. Desmarais asked her to call him back into the house.

"Mr. Beattie," he is reported to have said, "there won't be any bus service tomorrow to Copper Cliff. I need $3,000 to pay some wages, otherwise I'm dead." Beattie said: "What's the meaning of calling me at this time? I can't be giving you $3,000. You have to find a permanent solution to these problems. We can't carry on like this."

Desmarais then replied: "I'm sorry, but you're my last hope. I haven't got a chance unless you're willing to give it to me and then we'll try to work something out." Beattie told him: "You've got to work something out with the creditors and once you do that, once you have a formula, come and see me and we'll see what we can do about it. But meanwhile, I'll give you $3,000."[7] Desmarais soon came up with a financial solution acceptable both to his creditors and to Inco, thus putting the bus company back on a sound footing.

Desmarais then went to Ottawa and bought Gatineau Bus Lines. From there he picked up Quebec Auto Bus in Quebec City and Provincial Transport in Montreal. The move to Montreal in 1960 was a turning point for Desmarais: as a French Canadian he saw Quebec as a home away from home and as a source of strength. "French Canadians who feel in any way threatened have always looked to Quebec," he said. "It's part of their consciousness and it was part of mine." The purchase of *La Presse* in 1967 was an important decision for Desmarais, who wanted to put down roots in Quebec and be accepted as a member of the francophone elite. Nationalism was on the rise, Desmarais was a committed federalist, and he wanted to assure that the Montreal daily newspaper remained committed to national unity.

It took Desmarais ten years from the time he arrived in Montreal to build his various business ventures into a corporate empire. With the help of his brother Louis and Jean Parisien, both of whom had been with him from his beginnings in Sudbury, Desmarais bought a number of French newspapers in Quebec, expanded into the financial world, and moved into the recreational field. His stock-in-trade became the fish-swallowing-the-whale technique — the reverse takeover. Using this tactic, the target company in effect willingly pays for its own demise. Desmarais sells the assets of a company he owns to a firm he wants to acquire. Then he uses the proceeds from the sale to buy up the target company's own stocks. Through such complicated financial manoeuvring, Desmarais crept up the ladder of Canadian financial power.

In 1968 he took the biggest financial jump of his career when his umbrella organization, Trans-Canada Corporation, merged with Power Corporation, which had been controlled by the Montreal investment house of Nesbitt, Thomson. Desmarais became chief executive officer but shared control with Power's Peter Thomson. Two years later, he took over completely and Jean Parisien became president. Since then, Power Corporation has expanded to the point where it now manages $8 billion worth of assets and is one of the most important business conglomerates in Canada.

What makes Desmarais and Campeau different from French Quebecers of their generation is their strong desire to push their way into big business. They have never believed that French and English should occupy separate domains. Until recently in Quebec, the two language groups functioned according to a tacit understanding: the English ran business and the French controlled government and culture. There are complex historical reasons for this agreement, which did not completely collapse until the Parti Québécois came to power in 1976.[8] Desmarais and Campeau have never even subconsciously subscribed to this view of society. Though there have always been a sizeable minority of people in

Quebec who think like the two Franco-Ontarian businessmen, none seem capable of the same broad sweep across the country.

The Sudbury background of the two men has greatly contributed to their success as businessmen by giving them unusual cultural flexibility. Sudbury is in many ways a microcosm of Canada with its blend of French, English, and ethnic populations. People from the various communities are forced to come to terms with one another. In Quebec the two solitudes encourage people to see one another almost exclusively in term of stereotypes. Now that the English and French domains are dissolving in Quebec, there is more contact between the two groups, but polarization still exists. Tensions also prevail between the communities in Sudbury, but people there must adjust to one another.

"When I was a kid we had to learn how to get along," said Desmarais. "I went to a French school, but we saw English, Italians, Finns—people of different backgrounds—all the time." While Desmarais and Campeau were growing up, they learned how to function in more than one cultural world. The English did not terrify them. Without being aware of it, they became bilingual and, more importantly, bicultural. When they established themselves in Montreal and Ottawa, they carried with them their ability to deal in French and English circles. The frontier mentality of Sudbury also helped them. In Nouvel-Ontario there are no strong traditions, no set ways of doing things: what counts is the capacity to build and create from scratch.

Desmarais and Campeau, however, have always been conscious of the fact that the economic system is not culturally open. They are not afraid of the English because they talk their language and know how to gain entry into their banks for loans. But from the beginning, they realized it would take time to be accepted as equals. This influenced their style and the choices they made as businessmen.

Both grasped from the start that as French Canadians they would get nowhere trying to reach the top by joining national corporations. In their view, the top rungs of the corporate ladder were closed to people who did not belong to the English charter group. As a result, they opted to become owner-managers, rather than professional or hired managers. "Tell me," challenged Desmarais, "how long would it take a French Canadian to rise to the top of Sun Life? Pretty damn long." Desmarais always knew he must own, and not simply manage. "Of course, not everyone can be an owner," he said. "Some people should try to become presidents of corporations ... de Grandpré was successful at this at Bell. But in my view, ownership is the key to power. French Canadians have not been able to think of the long-term in business because they've had no economic power. That," he said, "is what must change."

In the predominantly English business world, neither Desmarais nor Campeau encountered problems until they tried to break into the top English institutional networks. The banks, they claim, have never discriminated against them. Desmarais ran into problems when he tried to take over Argus in 1975. He began eyeing the Toronto-based conglomerate in 1969 when he developed a beach-head as a stockholder with a 10 per cent interest. E.P. Taylor, who controlled Argus, regarded Desmarais as a protégé and indicated that eventually he might let him take Argus over. But by 1975 Bud McDougald was in control—and he was not interested in relinquishing power to a newcomer from Sudbury. Like Kenneth White at Royal Trustco, McDougald made agreements with various shareholders not to let Desmarais in. Desmarais managed to gain equity control, but not voting control. Although he secured a major chunk of stock, he was not invited to join the board of directors and eventually sold out at an estimated loss to Power Corporation of $2 million.

Both Desmarais and Campeau seem to relish testing just how far they can make the system bend in their direction. In their ambition and their predilection for risk-taking, they have more in common with swashbuckling American entrepreneurs than with their more bureaucratic and defensive Canadian colleagues.

Desmarais has been the subject of two commissions of inquiry. The first was conducted by the National Assembly in Quebec when he tried to buy Le Soleil in 1973. The government felt Desmarais controlled too much of the Quebec media and opposed his move to take charge of the Quebec City daily. Later, when Desmarais tried to take over Argus, the federal government set up the Bryce Commission to study the concentration of power in Canada's private sector.

Desmarais showed more caution in his dealings with Canadian Pacific Ltd. in late 1981. It was mutually understood that Power Corporation would not seek to acquire control of CP; its participation would not exceed 15 per cent, a figure which would still make Power the most important shareholder. In addition, Desmarais would be invited to sit on CP's executive council and as many as three "allies" would become members of the board. The agreement was worded to allow Power to increase its participation in Canadian Pacific should a third party launch a takeover bid.

This agreement with CP confirmed Desmarais's entry into the inner core of Canada's financial establishment. It was a compromise between the old guard and a new generation whose members often come from outside the traditional English-Protestant elite. And the manner in which it was done constituted tremendous progress over the earlier Argus and Royal Trustco ventures.

Desmarais's entry into Canadian Pacific was preceded by a major realignment of Power Corporation's portfolio. All assets in the field of transportation were liquidated. Shortly thereafter, with the help of Belgian, Swedish, and American interests, Power Corporation participated in the consolidation of the foreign assets of the Banque de Paris et des Pays Bas, which the French government was proposing to nationalize. Through Paribas Suisse and Pargesa Holding, Desmarais acquired a valuable entry in European financial circles, an interesting asset for Canadian Pacific.

Desmarais and Campeau are bicultural people—hybrids, so to speak. As such they are not entirely accepted by either the French or English communities. The price they pay for their ability to manoeuvre in two languages in the Canadian economy is that they are perceived as marginal—even tainted—by both cultures.[9]

Although they possess an English dimension, Desmarais and Campeau see themselves as primarily French. Both are sensitive to the problems of francophones across Canada. When Campeau moved to Ottawa, he discovered that the French separate school system was operating on a considerably smaller tax base than the English one. He declared Campeau Corporation Catholic for tax purposes, and sold property to the French school system at considerably reduced rates. Desmarais does not like some elements of Bill 101, but he strongly supports francization of the work place in Quebec. He is also eager to encourage expansion of a French-speaking business class and backed francophone entrepreneurs such as Jacques Francoeur and Philippe de Gaspé Beaubien when they needed financing. Desmarais, in his early days, was supported by Jean-Louis Lévesque of New Brunswick when he needed financing for Provincial Transport.

The French in Quebec have come to take pride in the achievements of Desmarais and Campeau, but they have not always felt this way. Until recently, Desmarais was considered a somewhat suspicious outsider by many francophones in Quebec. His frankly capitalist outlook, his life-style, his mixed group of English and French friends, and his Franco-Ontarian origins marked him as different. During the strike at *La Presse* in 1971, and later during the rise of radical leftist elements in the unions and community groups, Desmarais was regularly singled out as a grabby capitalist and exploiter. In strongly nationalist circles, he was fingered as an enemy of the Quebec people.

Anglophones, on the other hand, find Desmarais and Campeau hard to fathom. The economic interests and behaviour of the two men are still closer to the English than to the French, but some members of the old English establishment find them too aggressive. In both English and French Canada, Desmarais and Campeau continue to challenge the established order.

Desmarais and Campeau are the first important models for a new, more culturally flexible entrepreneurial class capable of doing business in two languages and two different milieus across the country. It is no accident that they came from the frontier town of Sudbury and not from Montreal or Toronto. Desmarais and Campeau are firmly challenging old ideas about roles and domains for English and French. Through their example, they are helping to break down the historic polarization of the two language groups in Canada. In their train are young people from Quebec, Ontario, and the West who recognize the duality of Canada and who pride themselves on being able to communicate in both languages.

Epilogue
The French Connection

Until the 1970s French communities like those in Nouvel-Ontario were of little more than folkloric interest to either Quebec or English Canada. This was mostly because the people in them were closed off from industrial society in rural parishes, unable to participate in the economic or political mainstream of the country. As people migrated from the country to the city, however, francophones outside Quebec developed an urban consciousness. This has improved their socio-economic status, which in turn is having important repercussions on present relationships between the English and French in Canada.

In Ontario a new French middle class that contrasts sharply with the traditional elite is starting to become involved in business, science, and technology. Through its example, more members of the Franco-Ontarian community are becoming full-fledged citizens capable of participating in a complete range of economic activities.

This middle class began to develop in the late 1960s, when French high schools opened in Ontario and French programs in colleges and universities expanded. Until then, many francophones dropped out of school in grade eight when they finished elementary school. The extension of French education has opened new horizons for Franco-Ontarians and made them more atune to the idea of careers in business and technology.

The passage of the Official Languages Act in 1969 and the increased use of French in the federal civil service have also paved the way for a more enterprising Franco-Ontarian middle class. Official bilingualism has given Franco-Ontarians a feeling of legitimacy and optimism. More importantly, it has given them the confidence they lacked to enter sectors of the economy from which they have always felt excluded.

The new business and commercial elite of Franco-Ontario is still in its early stages of development. It was only in 1981, for example, that a French businessmen's organization, the Cercle d'hommes d'affaires, was set up in Ontario. Unlike the Club Richelieu, which is more of a social club for businessmen and people in the professions, the Cercle d'hommes d'affaires is organized like a real chamber of commerce. It has branches in Ottawa and Sudbury and is branching out into other cities in Ontario with large francophone populations.

The new commercial class seems to be moving in two directions. It is eager to develop a French business network in Ontario with links to Quebec, but it is also willing to do business in English. As this new middle class grows, its special expertise, that comes from a knowledge of both languages and cultures, will become precious to both the English in Ontario and the French in Quebec. As the French language penetrates more and more into the infrastructure of the Canadian economy, these bilingual francophone businessmen will become increasingly important.

The large Canadian corporations with head offices in Toronto will want to use the Franco-Ontarians as intermediaries in their relations with their Quebec branches. But the Franco-Ontarians will become even more valuable to the growing numbers of Quebec companies that are trying to develop markets in the English provinces.

Quebecers have always tended to dismiss the francophones outside Quebec as a negligible force. Since 1977, however, the Quebec government has, for moral and cultural reasons, been giving large amounts of money to the Fédération des francophones hors Québec and holding regular meetings with organizations such as the Association canadienne-française de l'Ontario. The government feels it must support the demands of the French communities outside Quebec for increased rights. But it tends to measure their development in terms of the expansion of community and artistic activities; it finds it difficult to admit that progress could be seen in other terms, for example, through an economic infrastructure that could eventually benefit Quebecers as much as Franco-Ontarians.

The economy of Montreal, which entered a period of stagnation in the 1970s, is undergoing transformations that will be apparent later in the eighties. Economic studies show that productivity in certain key industries is progressing more rapidly in Quebec than in Ontario. The English-speaking head offices of the national companies are leaving Montreal for Toronto, but the vacuum is being filled by francophone entrepreneurs and administrators. With their own firms, they are penetrating the markets of the other provinces and developing fruitful relationships with companies outside Quebec. As the French economic class in Montreal expands further, the Franco-Ontarian commercial elite could become a key part of "the French connection" in the Canadian economy.

It seems clear that for the foreseeable future, Quebecers will not opt to become a separate country. If Quebec wants to maintain its weight within Canada, the government will without doubt expect the new generation of Quebec businessmen to expand its activities. But affirmation of the French fact in the Canadian economy cannot be realized without the integration of the minorities like the Franco-Ontarians and the Acadians—that is to say, their economic elites—into the financial and commercial network of the country. However, before this can be done, Quebecers must recognize that the French outside the province have a contribution to make to *la francophonie* that goes beyond folklore.

Appendix
The Marginal Man

Literature in the fields of sociology and history on the subject of
hybrids or culturally marginal people can be used to explain the
significance of Campeau, Desmarais, and other bicultural Franco-
Ontarians at this juncture of Canada's development as a two-
nation state.

The "marginal man," as sociologists have defined the concept, is
a member of a cultural, racial, or linguistic minority who is forced
to relate to the majority. By so doing, he becomes a hybrid, participating in both cultures without belonging completely to either
one.

The German sociologist Georg Simmel,[1] at the turn of the century, was the first to discuss the importance of the marginal man,
or "the stranger" as he referred to him, in mixed nation-states.
Simmel created his theories after observing the intermingling of
peoples and cultural groups in Europe as a result of migrations
and changes in political boundaries. The American sociologist
Robert Park, who was a follower of Simmel, explained the arrival
of the marginal man in this way:

> The vast expansion of Europe during the last 400 years brought about
> changes more devastating than in any earlier period in the world's
> history. Europeans have invaded every part of the world and no part of
> the earth has escaped the disturbing, even if vivifying, contacts of

European commerce and culture. The movements and migrations incident to this expansion have brought about everywhere an interpenetration of peoples and a fusion of cultures. Incidentally, it has produced at certain times and under certain conditions, a personality type which, if not wholly new, is at any rate peculiarly characteristic of the modern world. It is a type which some of us have given the title "the marginal man."[2]

The marginal man is an indispensable person in contacts between cultural groups as new nations develop. What the marginal man possesses that the homogeneous man does not is the capacity to step outside the confines of a particular culture or world-view. This allows him to easily reject behaviour patterns that are not suitable to new social and political situations.

Writing about the same time as Simmel and Park, historian Frederick J. Teggart described the marginal man as essential to the advancement of peoples.

Now, while historically, advancement has been dependent upon the collision of groups, the resultant response has taken place in the minds of individuals and so we are led to see that all transitional eras are alike in being periods of individual mental awakening, and of the release or emancipation of individual initiative in thought and action.[3]

Members of political and social subgroups can also be thought of as marginal men. Historian Arnold Toynbee discovered that men such as St. Paul, Buddha, and Lenin who led important movements gained the critical powers necessary for their actions by stepping outside of the boundaries of their particular cultures.[4]

Not all marginal men enjoy living in the ambivalent and often confusing world of two or more cultures. Many people need the comfort and security of strong roots and a single cultural resting place. Simmel celebrates the creative powers of the marginal man, but other sociologists such as Everett Stonequist[5] dwelt upon the social dislocation and permanent discomfort experienced by some of these personalities.

Positive and negative aspects of marginality can be seen wherever there are minglings of races and peoples. First generation immigrants in North America, francophones in Ontario, and now anglophones in Quebec have widely ranging reactions to this state of being. Some hybrid personalities are divided selves caught between two worlds. Others have been able to shed the burdensome aspects of both groups to create a new cultural model appropriate to the changing times.

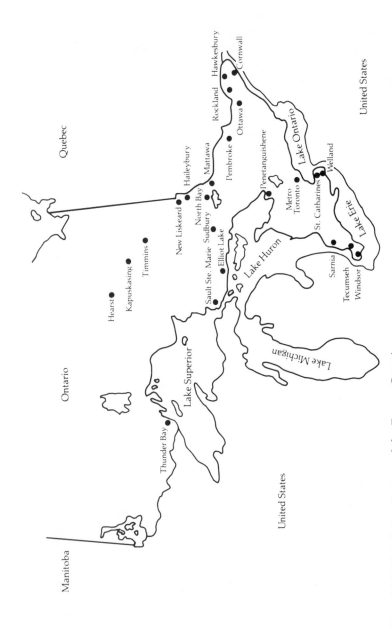

Map 1 Main Population Centres of the Franco-Ontarians

SOURCE: Conseil des affaires franco-ontariens, *Les Franco-Ontariens* (Toronto: Conseil des affaires franco-ontariens. 1979). pp. 2–3.

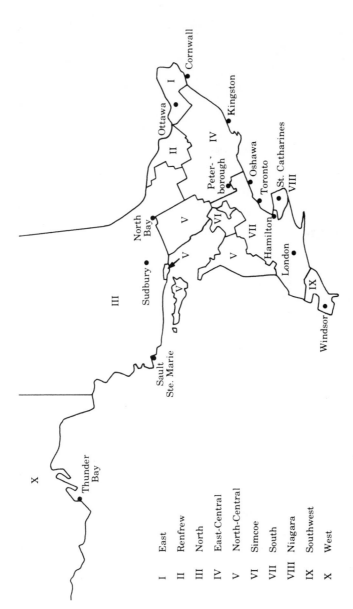

Map 2 The Ten Subregions of Ontario

SOURCE: Richard Joy, *Canada's Official-Language Minorities* (Montreal: C.D. Howe Research Institute, 1978), p. 17.

I   East
II   Renfrew
III   North
IV   East-Central
V   North-Central
VI   Simcoe
VII   South
VIII   Niagara
IX   Southwest
X   West

TABLE 1

Distribution of the French Population Outside of Quebec in 1971

Province	French Ethnic Origin	French Mother Tongue	French Home Language
Newfoundland	15,410	3,640	2,295
Prince Edward Island	15,325	7,360	4,410
Nova Scotia	80,220	39,335	27,215
New Brunswick	235,025	215,725	199,085
Ontario	737,360	482,040	352,465
Manitoba	86,510	60,545	39,600
Saskatchewan	56,200	31,605	15,935
Alberta	94,665	46,500	22,695
British Columbia	96,550	38,035	11,510
Total	1,417,265	924,790	675,210

SOURCE: Fédération des francophones hors Québec, *Les héritiers de Lord Durham*, vol. 1 (Ottawa: Fédération des francophones hors Québec, 1977), p. 23.

TABLE 2
Distribution of the French-Speaking Population of Ontario in 1971

Subregion	Total Population	Percentage Speaking French as a Home Language[1]	Percentage Speaking French as a Minor Language[2]	Total Percentage Speaking French[3]
East	596,000	24.0	13.2	37.1
Renfrew	91,000	2.5	6.8	9.3
North	541,000	25.1	10.8	35.8
East-Central	563,000	.6	3.7	4.3
North-Central	240,000	.4	2.5	2.9
Simcoe	171,000	2.2	5.7	7.9
South	4,521,000	.7	4.8	5.5
Niagara	347,000	3.2	5.0	8.2
Southwest	408,000	3.6	8.0	11.6
West	224,000	2.1	5.0	7.0
Ontario	7,703,000	4.6	5.9	10.5

SOURCE: 1971 census, cited in Richard Joy, *Canada's Official-Language Minorities* (Montreal: C.D. Howe Research Institute, 1978), p. 18.
1. Percentage of the population of each subregion replying "French" to the census question: "What language do you most often speak at home now?"
2. Percentage claiming an ability to carry on a conversation in French, less that shown under "home language."
3. Owing to rounding off of figures, the two components may not add up exactly to the total shown.

TABLE 3

Growth and Distribution of the Population of French Origin in Ontario[1]

Subregion	Percentage of the Total Population of French Origin[2]		Percentage Growth in the French Population[3]
	1941	1971	
East	33.2	25.9	54
Renfrew	2.2	1.7	50
North	28.1	26.4	86
East-Central	4.6	4.0	71
North-Central	2.1	1.1	7
Simcoe	2.5	2.2	76
South	10.7	22.5	314
Niagara	1.7	3.8	341
Southwest	12.4	9.6	54
West	2.5	2.8	117
Ontario	100.0	100.0	97

SOURCE: 1941 and 1971 census, cited in Richard Joy, *Canada's Official-Language Minorities* (Montreal: C.D. Howe Research Institute, 1978), p. 20.

1. In 1941 there were 373,990 persons of French origin in Ontario. In 1971 there were 737,360, an increase of 97 per cent. As the population of French origin in Quebec increased by only 77 per cent between 1941 and 1971, there would appear to have been a net migration into Ontario during the thirty-year period.
2. Computed as a percentage, in each region, of the total population of Ontario.
3. Actual growth in the population of French origin between 1941 and 1971, divided by the population in 1941.

TABLE 4
Effects of Assimilation in Ontario in 1971
(Number of persons of French origin who retain French
as their mother tongue and use French at home.)

Subregion	French Ethnic Origin	French Mother Tongue	French Home Language	French Home Language as Percentage of French Origin[1]
East	190,695	162,980	142,870	75
Renfrew	12.455	4,770	2,285	18
North	195,065	162,350	135,575	70
East-Central	29,620	8,620	3,520	12
North-Central	8,435	2,800	1,035	12
Simcoe	16,070	7,895	3,780	24
South	165,740	74,735	33,205	20
Niagara	27,845	17,110	11,010	40
Southwest	71,140	31,440	14,500	20
West	20,300	9,340	4,660	23
Ontario	737,360	482,045	352,465	48

SOURCE: 1971 census, cited in Richard Joy, *Canada's Official-Language Minorities* (Montreal: C.D. Howe Research Institute, 1978), p. 19.
1. The ratio of home language to ethnic origin indicates how well French has been retained. In Quebec, by comparison, the ratio is over 100 per cent because more people use French in their homes than are of French origin.

TABLE 5
Rate of Anglicization in Northern Ontario in 1971

County	Total Population	French Mother Tongue		French Home Language		Rate of Anglicization[1]
		Number	Percentage	Number	Percentage	
Algoma	121,935	12,650	10.4	8,450	6.9	33.2
Cochrane	95,835	47,225	49.3	42,835	44.7	9.3
Nipissing	78,870	25,890	32.8	21,430	27.2	17.2
Sudbury	198,075	64,035	32.3	52,175	26.3	18.5
Timiskaming	46,485	12,975	27.9	10,685	23.0	17.6
Total	541,200	162,775		135,575		

SOURCE: 1971 census, cited in Charles Castonguay, "Aperçu démolinguistique de la francophonie ontarienne," Bulletin du Centre de recherche en civilisation canadienne-française, University of Ottawa, 1977. Table 13.
1. Rate of anglicization: French mother tongue − French as a home language
$$\frac{\text{French mother tongue} - \text{French as a home language}}{\text{French mother tongue}}$$

TABLE 6

Comparison of the Education Levels Attained by
Franco-Ontarians and Ontarians in General

Level of Education	Percentage of Franco-Ontarians[1]	Percentage of Ontarians in General[2]
Masters or doctorate	0.8	1.1
Other university degree	2.2	4.0
Some university	3.9	5.0
Grade 13	3.6	8.9
Grade 12	11.4	16.0
Grade 11	7.2	9.2
Grades 9 and 10	24.2	23.0
Grades 5 to 8	38.1	27.2
Less than grade 4	8.6	5.6

SOURCE: Fédération des francophones hors Québec, *Les héritiers de Lord Durham*, vol. 1 (Ottawa: Fédération des francophones hors Québec, 1977), p. 38.

1. People of French mother tongue, age fifteen and over, who were not full-time students at the time of the survey. Total sample: 311,710.
2. Total sample: 4,766,010.

TABLE 7

Comparison of Income Levels Attained by
Franco-Ontarians and Ontarians in General

Income Level	Percentage of Franco-Ontarians[1]	Percentage of Ontarians in General[2]
Without Income	25.4	20.5
$1,000 or less	10.2	12.4
$1,000–$2,999	19.9	18.1
$3,000–$4,999	12.6	13.0
$5,000–$6,999	12.0	12.1
$7,000–$8,999	10.3	10.0
$9,000–$10,999	6.0	6.1
$11,000–$12,999	2.6	3.0
$13,000–$14,999	1.2	1.5
$15,000–$19,999	1.7	1.8
$20,000–$24,999	1.4	0.6
$25,000 and up	0.5	0.9

SOURCE: Fédération des francophones hors Québec. *Les héritiers de Lord Durham*, vol. 1 (Ottawa: Fédération des francophones hors Québec, 1977), p. 35.

1. People of French mother tongue, age fifteen and over. Total sample: 351,915.
2. Total sample: 5,495,910.

TABLE 8

Comparison of the Economic Activities of Franco-Ontarians and Ontarians in General

Economic Activity	Ontario		North-East Ontario	
	Percentage of Total Population	Percentage of French Mother Tongue	Percentage of Total Population	Percentage of French Mother Tongue
Agriculture	4	3	2	1
Forestry, hunting, fishing, mines	1	6	13	17
Manufacturing	24	20	16	15
Construction and public works	6	8	6	9
Transport, communication	6	6	8	7
Commerce	15	14	14	13
Finance, insurance, and real estate	5	2	4	3
Socio-cultural, commercial, and personal services	23	20	22	20
Public administration and defence	8	11	8	6
Indefinite	8	10	7	9
Primary Sector	5	10	10	20
Secondary Sector	32	30	25	35
Tertiary Sector	63	60	55	45

SOURCE: Gaétan Vallières and Marcien Villemure, *Atlas de l'Ontario français* (Montreal: Études Vivantes, 1981), pp. 56–57.

TABLE 9

Rate of Mixed Marriages Outside of Quebec
(Percentage of the population of French mother tongue
who marry English spouses.)

Province	Men	Women
Newfoundland	45.5	38.0
Prince Edward Island	23.6	28.7
Nova Scotia	32.6	32.1
New Brunswick	9.1	10.9
Ontario	28.9	30.4
Manitoba	32.4	32.8
Saskatchewan	42.3	42.0
Alberta	47.3	47.6
British Columbia	61.1	58.5

SOURCE: Fédération des francophones hors Québec,
Les héritiers de Lord Durham, vol. 1 (Ottawa: Fédération des francophones hors Québec, 1977), p. 33.

TABLE 10

Loss of French in Mixed Marriages Outside Quebec
(Percentage of francophones in mixed marriages
who use English at home.)

Province	Francophones Using English at Home
Newfoundland	90.1
Prince Edward Island	95.8
Nova Scotia	93.1
New Brunswick	82.6
Ontario	92.0
Manitoba	94.9
Saskatchewan	96.3
Alberta	96.2
British Columbia	97.4

SOURCE: Fédération des francophones hors Québec,
Les héritiers de Lord Durham, vol. 1 (Ottawa: Fédération des francophones hors Québec, 1977), p. 33.

Notes

Chapter 1

1. Robert Dickson, *Au nord de notre vie*, poster poem (Sudbury: Prise de Parole, 1975). Translated here by Susan Blaylock. Original as follows:

   Au nord de notre vie
       ICI
   où la distance use les cœurs pleins
   de la tendresse minerai de la
   terre de pierre de forêts et de froid
       NOUS
   têtus souterrains et solidaires
   lâchons nos cris rauques et rocheux
   aux quatre vents
   de l'avenir possible

2. La Corvée, *La parole et la loi* (Sudbury: Prise de Parole, 1980), p. 61. Translated here by Susan Blaylock. Original as follows:

   L'histoire, c'est à chacun d'la faire,
   On est tanné d'être des minoritaires
   Des temps passés, des temps présents,
   On a le goût de regarder devant!

   A force de chercher notre identité
   On est p'us capable, même de respirer.
   Parlez-nous p'us d'assimilation,
   Ni de peuple en voie d'extinction.

On voulait vous dire les luttes du passé.
Pour ceux qui connaissent pas et ceux qui ont oublié
Dans le prochain spectacle, on parlera p'us d'histoire.
On espère que vous s'rez là pour le voir!

3. Jean-Marc Dalpé, *Les murs de nos villages* (Sudbury: Prise de Parole, 1980), p. 42. Translated here by the author. Original as follows:

Les murs de nos villages se souviennent
Les murs de nos villages se rappellent
nos racines dans ce pays
aussi creuses que celles d'un vieux chêne

....

Les violons de nos villages
nous hurlent des gigues assoiffées de Liberté
et qui ne veulent dire qu'une chose:
Icitte c'est chez nous.

4. The education provisions under Article 23 of the Charter of Rights in the Canadian constitution do not, in the opinion of francophones outside Quebec, sufficiently protect them. It offers them French classes "where numbers warrant" but does not guarantee them a basic and inalienable right to French education.
5. Ronald Sutherland, *Second Image*, p. 29.
6. Ibid., p. 44.
7. Ibid., p. 42.

Chapter 2

1. André Paiement, *Mon Pays*, recorded by CANO on *Au nord de notre vie* (A&M Records, 1977). Translated here by Dominique Clift. Original lyrics as follows:

Mon moulin
Mon village
Mes trois amis
Mes deux langues
Quand mon pays était un paysage
Bien en vie
Sans âge

Un son de cloche
Ne dit pas notre chanson
Sa distance est son courage
Aujourd'hui sans boussole pour nous guider
On se lance à l'abordage.

2. Germain Lemieux, *Les vieux m'ont conté* (Montreal: Éditions Bellarmin, vols. 1–17: 1973–1981; vols. 18–30: forthcoming).

3. André Paiement, *La vie et les temps de Médéric Boileau* (Sudbury: Prise de Parole, 1978), p. 42. Translated here by Susan Blaylock. Original as follows:

Le vieux Médéric
Vient de sortir du bois
Le vieux Médéric
J'pense qu'y comprend pas

Hé St-Pierre de Porquépique
De St-Herménégilde
Le vieux Médéric Boileau
Vient d'arriver en ville!

. . . .

Cinquante ans dans le bois
Et c'est difficile
Pour un vieux comme lui
De comprendre la ville ...

4. Malcolm Reid, "A Different Chanson," p. 82. Italics in original.
5. *Joual,* a corruption of the French word *cheval,* is a term used in Quebec to describe a dialect that employs large amounts of slang and English.
6. Paiement, *Médéric Boileau,* p. 13. Translated here by Robert Dickson. Original as follows:

Les soirées d'hiver
C'était donc tranquille
Tout ce qu'y avait à faire
C'était de s'asseoir

Pour écouter la grosse truie
Qui ronflait
Qui nous réchauffait
L'hiver a toujours été
Ce que j'ai préféré

7. Jean-Guy Pilon, "Je murmure le nom de mon pays," in *Modern Canadian Verse,* ed. A.J.M. Smith (Toronto: Oxford University Press, 1967), p. 324. Translated here by Susan Blaylock. Original as follows:

Je murmure le nom de mon pays
Comme un secret obscène
Ou une plaie cachée
Sur mon âme
Et je ne sais plus
La provenance des vents
Le dessin des frontières
Ni l'amorce des villes

Un matin comme un enfant
A la fin d'un trop long voyage
Nous ouvrirons des bras nouveaux
Sur une terre habitable
Sans avoir honte d'en dire le nom
Qui ne sera plus murmuré
Mais proclamé

Chapter 4

1. Quoted in Paul-François Sylvestre, *Penetang: L'école de la résistance* (Sudbury: Prise de Parole, 1980), pp. 21, 73. Translated here by Sheila McLeod Arnopoulos.
2. The Franco-Ontarian flag was first flown on September 25, 1975, in Sudbury. It combines the French *fleur de lis* and the trillium, Ontario's provincial flower.
3. Quoted in Sylvestre, *Penetang*, p. 22. Translated here by Susan Blaylock.
4. Ibid., p. 22.
5. Ibid.
6. La Corvée, *La parole et la loi* (Sudbury: Prise de Parole, 1980), p. 25. Translated here by Susan Blaylock. Italics added. (This is not a verbatim quotation from any speech by Premier William Davis.)
7. Ibid., p. 34.
8. For a detailed comparison of the French in Quebec and the French in Ontario, see Danielle Juteau-Lee, "Français d'Amérique, Canadiens, Canadiens-Français, Franco-Ontariens, Ontarois: qui sommes-nous?" *Pluriel* (Paris) 24 (1980): 21–42.
9. Franklin A. Walker, *Catholic Education and Politics in Ontario*, pp. 4, 5.
10. An excellent treatment of the problem can be found in Clinton Archibald, "La Pensée politique des Franco-Ontariens au XXe siècle," in *Revue du Nouvel-Ontario*, no. 2 (Sudbury: l'Institut Franco-Ontarien, 1979), pp. 13–30.
11. René Brodeur and Robert Choquette, *Villages et visages de l'Ontario français*, p. 18.
12. Robert Choquette, *Language and Religion*.
13. Conflict between the Protestants and Catholics in Ontario began much earlier, but subsided during the pre-Confederation period. For a detailed discussion of Protestant opposition to Catholic schools in the 1850s, see Franklin A. Walker, *Catholic Education and Politics in Upper Canada* (Toronto: J.M. Dent and Sons, 1955).
14. Choquette, *Language and Religion*, p. 250.
15. Ibid., p. 56.
16. Ibid., p. 73.
17. Marilyn Barber, "The Ontario Bilingual Schools Issue: Sources of Conflict," in *Minorities, Schools and Politics*, ed. Ramsay Cook, Craig Brown, and Carl Berger (Toronto: University of Toronto Press, 1969), p. 79.

18. Michel Renouf, "Ah! Ils sont sortis! ..." *La Revue franco-améri-caine* 5 (Nov. 1, 1910): 25.
19. For an account of reactions to Regulation 17 in Ontario and Quebec, see Margaret Prang, "Clerics, Politicians, and the Bilingual Schools Issue in Ontario, 1910–1917," in *Minorities, Schools, and Politics,* ed. Ramsay Cook, Craig Brown, and Carl Berger.
20. Choquette, *Language and Religion,* p. 231.
21. Ibid., p. 243.
22. Ibid., p. 231.
23. Choquette, *Language and Religion,* chapter 1; and Marilyn Barber, "The Ontario Bilingual Schools Issue."
24. Choquette, *Language and Religion,* p. 223.
25. For more details, see T.H.B. Symons, "Ontario's Quiet Revolution," p. 178.
26. A similar position was taken by the Hall-Dennis Commission. See Justice E.M. Hall et al., *Living and Learning: The Report of the Provincial Committee on Aims and Objectives of Education in the Schools of Ontario* (Toronto: Ontario Ministry of Education, 1968), p. 784.
27. Gérald Snow, *Les droits linguistiques des Acadiens du Nouveau-Brunswick,* p. 49.
28. In the north of Ontario as a whole, more than 50 per cent of the workers are miners, lumberjacks, skilled tradesmen, or labourers. Professionals make up 10 per cent of the work force, administrators 6 per cent, and businessmen 4 per cent. See Yvan Allaire and Jean-Marie Toulouse, *Situation socio-économique et satisfaction des chefs de ménage franco-ontariens,* p. 55.

Chapter 5

1. Robert Paris, *Le ou la Common Law.* Translated here by Sheila McLeod Arnopoulos.
2. *Globe and Mail,* national edition, May 14, 1981, p. 13.
3. For a more extensive discussion of this trend, see Omer Des-lauriers, "La situation de la vie franco-ontarienne," in *Revue du Nouvel-Ontario,* no. 1 (Sudbury: L'Institut franco-ontarien, 1978), p. 25.
4. Pierre Savard, "De la difficulté d'être franco-ontarien," in *Revue du Nouvel Ontario,* no. 1 (Sudbury: L'Institut franco-ontarien, 1978), p. 21. Translated here by Susan Blaylock.

Chapter 6

1. Patrice Desbiens, *l'espace qui reste* (Sudbury: Prise de Parole, 1979), p. 39. Translated here by the author. Original as follows:

   je suis la chérie
   canadienne.

je suis le franco-ontarien
dans le woolworth
abandonné de ses rêves

. . . .

des souvenirs de timmins
ontario adhère à mon
corps comme du
frimas.
des matantes et des mononcles
me tournent dans la tête
comme une veillée de
noël.
je vis à toronto ontario.
j'ai un larousse de poche
avec 32,000 mots.
je trébuche sur ma langue.
ma langue se détache de
ma bouche.
elle se tortille, elle frémit
comme un chien mourant
sur la rue yonge.
vive le québec libre.

vive le québec libre.
je suis la chérie
canadienne.
je suis le franco-ontarien
cherchant une sortie
d'urgence dans le
woolworth démoli
de ses rêves.

2. Sociologist Donald Dennis of Laurentian University points out
   some of the problems caused by the French elite's view of culture
   in "De la difficulté d'être idéologue franco-ontarien," in *Revue
   du Nouvel-Ontario*, no. 1 (Sudbury: L'Institut franco-ontarien,
   1978), p. 85.
3. This is also true of French youth in Quebec, though much less so.
   In Montreal, for example, one third of all television programs
   watched by French youth are in English. See Edith Bédard and
   Daniel Monnier, *Conscience linguistique des jeunes Québécois*,
   vol. 1, for the Conseil de la langue française (Quebec: Éditeur
   officiel du Québec, 1981), p. 51; and Pierre Georgeault, *Conscience
   linguistique des jeunes Québécois*, vol. 2, for the Conseil de la
   langue français (Quebec: Éditeur officiel du Québec, 1981).
4. Calvin Veltman, *The Assimilation of American Language Minorities: Structure, Pace, and Extent* (Washington: National Centre for
   Education and Welfare, 1979).

5. Richard Joy, *Canada's Official-Language Minorities* (Montreal: C.D. Howe Research Institute, 1978), p. 19.

6. Ibid., p. 18.

7. Pierre Savard, Rhéal Beauchamp, and Paul Thompson, *Arts With A Difference*, p. 16.

8. Charles Castonguay, "Aperçu démolinguistique de la francophonie ontarienne," tables 14 and 18.

9. Charles Castonguay, "Intermarriage and Language Shift in Canada, 1971 and 1976," Department of Mathematics, University of Ottawa, 1980, tables 1 and 2. These tables show that 90 per cent of mixed marriage couples in Ontario use English in the home. In Quebec, intermarriage is limited to only 3 per cent of the francophone population. Among mixed marriage couples in Quebec, 46 per cent use English, 36 per cent use French, and 17 per cent use both languages in the home.

10. For a more extensive treatment of this question see Hubert Guindon, "The Modernization of Quebec and the Legitimacy of the Federal State."

11. Joy, *Canada's Official-Language Minorities*, p. 16

12. Ibid., p. 20.

13. Pierre Savard, "De la difficulté d'être franco-ontarien," in *Revue du Nouvel-Ontario*, no. 1 (Sudbury: L'Institut franco-ontarien, 1978), p. 16. Translated here by Sheila McLeod Arnopoulos. The Superfrancofête was a huge cultural festival held in Quebec City in the mid-1970s that attracted francophone performers from French communities across Canada as well as from Quebec.

14. Joy, *Canada's Official-Language Minorities*, p. 8, table 3.

15. Pierre Savard, "De la difficulté d'être franco-ontarien," p. 11.

16. Pierre Savard, Rhéal Beauchamp, and Paul Thompson, *Arts With a Difference*, p. 49.

Chapter 7

1. Jean-Marc Dalpé, *Gens d'ici* (Sudbury: Prise de Parole, 1980), p. 58. Translated here by the author. Original as follows:

Au début du siècle, même un peu avant
Y débarquent du train parti de Trois-Rivières, de Montréal
du Lac St-Jean, de Québec ou de Gaspé
Y débarquent sans un sou
quelques mots d'anglais en poche
pis la mémoire des fêtes de famille
sur la terre paternelle en tête
Ramassent casques durs, chandelles, boussoles, pics, pelles
et se retrouvent bientôt
à quelques centaines de pieds sous terre
dans un monde sans jour
un monde de nuit et de sueur
avec par boutte la chaleur, par boutte le frette

toujours l'humidité, toujours le gôut de poussière à bouche
pis toujours le cri de douleur de l'autre
qui s'est fait piner dans un coin, hier
par un chariot déraillé

. . . .

L'Histoire, la nôtre
qui nous nourrit d'espoirs et de rêves
est celle de ces gens-là
et ces bras, de ces cœurs, de cette langue
plutôt que celle des Grands de ce monde

2. Officially known as the Joint Federal-Provincial Inquiry Commission into Safety in Mines and Mining Plants in Ontario.
3. For a detailed history of Mine-Mill, see John B. Lang, "A Lion in a Den of Daniels: A History of the International Union of Mine. Mill, and Smelter Workers in Sudbury, Ontario, 1942–1962." Unpublished M.A. thesis, University of Guelph, 1970.
4. W.E. Kon. "Boom Town into Company Town: The Story of Sudbury," New Frontier, 1936, p. 6.
5. Jim Tester, The Shaping of Sudbury: A Labour View (Sudbury: Local 598, Mine-Mill Union, 1980), p. 25.
6. During this period, much of the Canadian union movement was tied to American unions that were insensitive to Canadian issues. Mine-Mill was the first Canadian branch to successfully break away. For a history of the struggle to Canadianize the union movement. see Rick Salutin, Kent Rowley: The Organizer.
7. The Canadian Congress of Labor became the Canadian Labor Congress in 1956 when it joined the Trades and Labor Congress of Canada.
8. This later became the Confederation of Canadian Unions.
9. Proceedings and addresses of The Catholic Social Life Conference, Ottawa, 1959, p. 54.

Chapter 8

1. Jean-Marc Dalpé, Les murs de nos villages (Sudbury: Prise de Parole, 1980), p. 14. Translated here by the author. Original as follows:

Tu as le canard sauvage au front
tu tiens des tas d'hivers dans le creux de tes mains
tes bras sont gros commes des arbres que tu as abattus
ton visage marqué à coups de lames par le vent du Nord
rit plus fort que le cri du corbeau noir
ton cœur pompe le sang au rythme plein du rigodon
il y a un violon dans tes jambes quand tu danses
ta vie est de neige est de forêt est de sueur
quand tu t'y mets ta parole est poésie
tu a dompté un pays plus malin que le Diable
et quand tu t'y mets tu chantes ce pays en disant 'mon'

2. Jean-Marc Dalpé, "L'église," *Gens d'ici* (Sudbury: Prise de Parole, 1981), p. 31. Translated here by Susan Blaylock. Original as follows:

La construction de l'église
c'est comme si le village signait son nom sur le paysage
comme au bas d'un contrat avec le Créateur.

La fierté du village
comme une pierre précieuse
montée sur la plus haute colline
à la vue de tous, hommes, femmes, enfants
forêts ruisseaux et champs.

3. Jean-Marc Dalpé, "Hommes et femmes d'ici," in *Gens d'ici*, p. 17. Translated here by the author. Original as follows:

Vos yeux vêtus d'étendues de silence
nous parlent
du lien qu'on a avec la terre d'ici
et ses habits de saison
avec la rivière en débâcle, la forêt enneigée
et les champs à récolter

nous parlent
de notre lien de parenté
avec le loup, l'ours
le lièvre, la perdrix et l'hirondelle

avec tout ce qui pousse, tout ce qui bouge
tout ce qui respire

Hommes et femmes d'ici

notre Histoire est inscrite dans vos cœurs
et dans vos sourires

4. André Paiement, *La vie et les temps de Médéric Boileau* (Sudbury: Prise de Parole, 1978), p. 40. Translated here by Susan Blaylock.

Chapter 9

1. Peter C. Newman, *The Canadian Establishment*, vol. 2: *The Acquisitors* (Toronto: McClelland and Stewart, 1981), p. 11.
2. James Lorimer, *The Developers* (Toronto: James Lorimer and Company, 1978), p. 20.
3. Testimony before the Ontario Securities Commission, quoted in *Globe and Mail*, January 16, 1981.
4. Quoted in Graham Fraser and Patrick Howe, "The Real Man Behind Campeau The Gambler," *Globe and Mail*, June 19, 1975.
5. In Montreal, Westmount is the home of the wealthiest members of the traditional English elite.

6. Ronald Sutherland, *Second Image*.
7. Quoted in Peter Newman, *The Canadian Establishment*, vol. 1, p. 68.
8. For more on the English and French domains and their breakdown in the wake of the Quiet Revolution, see Sheila McLeod Arnopoulos and Dominique Clift, *The English Fact in Quebec*.
9. For some theoretical background on the role and nature of the hybrid, or bicultural, personality type which is discussed here and elsewhere in the book, see the Appendix.

Appendix

1. Georg Simmel, *Soziologie* (Leipzig: Dunker and Humlot, 1968).
2. Robert Park, Introduction to Everett Stonequist, *The Marginal Man: A Study of Personality and Culture Conflict* (New York: Russell and Russell, 1961), p. xiv.
3. Frederick Teggart, *Processes of History* (New Haven: Yale University Press, 1918), p. 155.
4. Arnold Toynbee, *A Study of History*, vol. 3 (London: Oxford University Press, 1934).
5. Everett Stonequist, *The Marginal Man*.

Bibliography and Suggested Readings

Allaire, Yvan, and Toulouse, Jean-Marie. *Situation socio-économique et satisfaction des chefs de ménage franco-ontariens.* Ottawa: Association canadienne-française de l'Ontario, 1973.

Arnopoulos, Sheila McLeod, and Clift, Dominique. *The English Fact in Quebec.* Montreal: McGill-Queen's University Press, 1980.

Atwood, Margaret. *Survival.* Toronto: House of Anansi Press, 1972.

Beattie, Christopher. *Minority Men in a Majority Setting.* Toronto: McClelland and Stewart, 1975.

Bériault, Roland. *Rapport du comité sur les écoles de langue française de l'Ontario.* Toronto: Department of Education, Government of Ontario, 1968.

Bordeleau, G., ed. *Educational and Vocational Plans of Franco-Ontarian Grade 12 and 13 Students in Ontario Schools, 1975–76.* Toronto: Ontario Advisory Council for Franco-Ontarian Affairs, 1976.

Brodeur, R., and Choquette, Robert. *Villages et visages de l'Ontario français.* Toronto and Montreal: L'Office de la télécommunication éducative de l'Ontario, in collaboration with Fides, 1979.

Canale, Michel, and Mougeon, Raymond. "Problèmes posés par la mesure du rendement en français des élèves franco-ontariens." In *Langue maternelle, langue première de communication?* edited by B. Cazabon. Sudbury: L'Institut franco-ontarien, Laurentian University, 1978.

Castonguay, Charles. "La montée de l'anglicisation chez les jeunes franco-ontariens." Bulletin du Centre de recherche en civilisation canadienne-française, University of Ottawa, 1976.

– "Aperçu démolinguistique de la francophonie ontarienne." Bulletin du Centre de recherche en civilisation canadienne-française, University of Ottawa, 1976.

- "L'ampleur des mariages mixtes chez les jeunes époux de langue maternelle française en Ontario et au Nouveau-Brunswick." Bulletin du Centre de recherche en civilisation canadienne-française, University of Ottawa, 1979.

Chaperon-Lor, Diane. *Une minorité s'explique.* Toronto: Institut d'études pédagogiques de l'Ontario, 1974.

Choquette, Robert. *Language and Religion: A History of English-French Conflict in Ontario.* Ottawa: University of Ottawa Press, 1975.

- "Remember French." In *How To Live In French In Ontario.* Toronto: Ontario Educational Communications Authority, 1978.

- *L'Ontario français, historique.* Montreal: Études Vivantes, 1982.

Clark, S.D. "The Position of the French-Speaking Population in the Northern Industrial Community." In *Canadian Society: Pluralism, Change, and Conflict,* edited by R.J. Ossenberg. Toronto: Prentice-Hall, 1971.

Cook, Ramsay; Brown, Craig; and Berger, Carl; eds. *Minorities, Schools, and Politics.* Toronto: University of Toronto Press, 1969.

Coons, W.H.; Taylor, Donald; and Tremblay, Marc-Adélard, eds. *The Individual, Language, and Society.* Ottawa: The Canada Council, 1978.

Elliott, J.L., ed. *Two Nations, Many Cultures: Ethnic Groups in Canada.* Toronto: Prentice-Hall, 1979.

Fédération des francophones hors Québec. *Les héritiers de Lord Durham.* Ottawa: Fédération des francophones hors Québec, 1977.

- *Deux poids deux mesures: les francophones hors Québec et les anglophones au Québec, un dossier comparatif.* Ottawa: Fédération des francophones hors Québec, 1978.

Fishman, Joshua. *The Sociology of Language.* Rawley, Mass.: Newbury House, 1972.

Godbout, Arthur. *L'origine des écoles françaises dans l'Ontario.* Ottawa: University of Ottawa Press, 1972.

Grimard, Jacques. *L'Ontario français par l'image.* Montreal: Etudes Vivantes, 1982.

Guindon, Hubert. "The Modernization of Quebec and the Legitimacy of the Canadian State." In *Modernization and the Canadian State,* edited by D. Glenday, H. Guindon, and A. Turowetz. Toronto: Macmillan, 1978.

Hébrard, P., and Mougeon, R. "La langue parlée entre les parents et les enfants: un facteur crucial dans l'acquisition linguistique de l'enfant dans un milieu bilingue." Mimeograph. Toronto: Centre d'études franco-ontariennes, Ontario Institute for Studies in Education, 1975.

Jackson, John. *Community and Conflict: A Study of English-French Relations in Ontario.* Toronto: Holt, Rinehart, and Winston, 1975.

Joy, Richard. *Language in Conflict.* Toronto: McClelland and Stewart, 1972.

- *Canada's Official-Language Minorities*. Montreal: C.D. Howe Research Institute, 1978.

Juteau-Lee, Danielle. "Français d'Amerique, Canadiens, Canadiens-Français, Franco-Ontariens, Ontarois: qui sommes-nous?" *Pluriel* 24 (1980): 21–42.

Juteau-Lee, Danielle, and Lapointe, Jean. "Identité culturelle et identité structurelle dans l'Ontario francophone: analyse d'une transition." *Actes du IIIe colloque consacré à l'identité culturelle et la francophonie dans les Amériques.* Quebec: Centre international de recherche sur le bilinguisme, Université Laval, 1978.

Lang, John B. "A Lion in a Den of Daniels: A History of the International Union of Mine, Mill, and Smelter Workers in Sudbury, Ontario, 1942–1962." Master's thesis, University of Guelph, 1970.

Lapierre, André. *La Toponymie française en Ontario.* Montreal: Études Vivantes, 1982.

Liaison. Franco-Ontarian literary review published by Les Éditions l'Interligne, Ottawa.

Lorimer, James. *The Developers.* Toronto: James Lorimer and Company, 1978.

Mackey, William F. "The Effects of Mixed French / English Schools: Assimilation or Bilingualism." *Language and Society* 4 (Winter 1981): 10–14.

Maxwell, Thomas. *The Invisible French: The French in Metropolitan Toronto.* Waterloo, Ont.: Wilfrid Laurier University Press, 1977.

Morris, Raymond N., and Lanphier, C. Michael. *Three Scales of Inequality: Perspectives on English-French Relations.* Toronto: Longmans Canada, 1977.

Mougeon, Raymond. "Bilingual Schools vs. French Language Schools: A Study of Parental Expectations Among French-Ontarians." Mimeograph. Toronto: Centre d'études franco-ontariennes, Ontario Institute for Studies in Education, 1978.

- "Assimilation des jeunes franco-ontariens en communauté minoritaire." Mimeograph. Toronto: Centre d'études franco-ontariennes, Ontario Institute for Studies in Education, 1979.

- "French Language Replacement and Mixed Marriages: The Case of the Francophone Minority of Welland, Ontario." *Anthropological Linguistics* 19 (9), 1977.

- "Le maintien du français en Ontario." Mimeograph. Toronto: Centre d'études franco-ontariennes, Ontario Institute for Studies in Education, 1976.

- "Les mariages mixtes et l'assimilation des francophones au Canada." *Revue de l'Association canadienne d'éducation de langue française* 8 (1), 1980.

Mougeon, Raymond; Brent-Palmer, C.; Bélanger, M.; and Cichocki, W. "Le français parlé en milieu scolaire dans des communautés franco-ontariennes minoritaires." Mimeograph. Toronto: Centre d'études franco-ontariennes, Ontario Institute for Studies in Education, 1980.

195

Mougeon, Raymond, and Canale, M. "A Linguistic Perspective on Ontarian French." *Canadian Journal of Education* 4 (4), 1979.

- "Apprentissage et enseignement du français dans les écoles de langue française de l'Ontario: français langue première ou langue seconde?" Mimeograph. Toronto: Centre d'études franco-ontariennes, Ontario Institute for Studies in Education, 1980.

- "Maintenance of French in Ontario: Is Education in French Enough?" *Interchange* 9 (4), 1979.

- "Minority Language Schooling in English Canada: The Case of the Franco-Ontarians." Mimeograph. Toronto: Centre d'études franco-ontariennes, Ontario Institute for Studies in Education, 1977.

Mougeon, Raymond; Canale, M.; and Bélanger, Monique. "Rôle de la société dans l'acquisition et le maintien du français par les élèves franco-ontariens." *Canadian Modern Language Review* 34 (3), 1978.

Mougeon, Raymond, and Hébrard, P. "Les chances de maintien du français en Ontario." *Courrier Sud* (Toronto) 3 (9), 1975.

Mougeon, Raymond; Savard, H.; and Carroll, S. "Le Cheval de Troie de l'assimilation à Welland: les mariages mixtes." *L'Express* (Toronto) 3 (42), 1978.

Newman, Peter. *The Canadian Establishment*, 2 vols. Toronto: McClelland and Stewart, 1975, 1981.

Oliver, Peter. "The Resolution of the Ontario Bilingual Schools Crisis: 1919, 1929." *Journal of Canadian Studies / Revues d'études canadiennes* February 1972: 22–45.

- "Cultural Strife and Ethnic Survival: The Franco-Ontarian Experience." In *Keeping Canada Together Means Changing Our Thinking*. Toronto: Amethyst Publications, 1978.

Paris, Robert. *Le ou la Common Law*. Quebec: Éditeur officiel du Québec, forthcoming.

Patry, Réjean M. *La législation linguistique fédérale*. Quebec: Éditeur officiel du Québec, 1981.

Ravault, René-Jean. "La francophonie clandestine, ou: De l'aide du Secrétariat d'État aux communautés francophones hors Québec de 1968 à 1976." Mimeograph. Toronto: Centre de recherche en civilisation canadienne-française, University of Ottawa, 1976.

Reid, Malcolm. "A Different Chanson." *Quest*, December 1981.

Revue du Nouvel-Ontario. no. 1, Les Franco-Ontariens à l'heure de l'indépendance, 1978; no. 2, Politique et syndicalisme: réalités négligées en Ontario français, 1979; no. 3, Les idéologies de l'Ontario français: un choix de textes (1912–1980), 1981. Sudbury: L'Institut franco-ontarien, Laurentian University.

Roberts, Stanley C. "Attitudes Towards Bilingualism: Starting Changes." *Language and Society* 4 (Winter 1981): 3–6.

Saint-Jacques, Bernard. *Aspects sociolinguistiques du bilinguisme canadien*. Quebec: Centre international de recherche sur le bilinguisme, Université Laval, 1976.

Salutin, Rick. *Kent Rowley: The Organizer.* Toronto: James Lorimer and Company, 1980.

Savard, Pierre; Beauchamp, Rhéal; and Thompson, Paul. *Arts With A Difference: A Report on French-Speaking Ontario.* Ottawa: Ontario Arts Council, 1977.

Sissons, C.B. *Bi-lingual Schools in Canada.* Toronto: Dent, 1917.

Snow, Gérard. *Les droits linguistiques des Acadiens du Nouveau-Brunswick.* Quebec: Éditeur officiel du Québec, 1981.

Stern, H.H. "Immersion Schools and Language Learning." *Language and Society* 5 (Spring, 1981): 3–6.

Sutherland, Ronald. *Second Image.* Toronto: New Press, 1971.

Symons, T.H.B. "Ontario's Quiet Revolution: A Study of Change in the Position of the Franco-Ontarian Community." In *One Country or Two?*, edited by R.M. Burns. Montreal: McGill-Queen's University Press, 1971.

Tissot, Georges. "Au-delà de la survivance: Pénétang et l'auto-détermination." *Liaison* 8 (Dec.–Jan. 1980).

Vallée, Frank G., and de Vries, John. "Issues and Trends in Bilingualism in Canada." In *Advances in the Study of Multilingual Societies,* edited by Joshua Fishman. The Hague: Mouton, 1973.

Vallières, Gaétan. *L'Ontario français par les documents.* Montreal: Études Vivantes, 1982.

Vallières, Gaétan, and Savard, Pierre. *La Voix de l'Ontario. Volume 1: 1913–1920; Volume 2: 1920–1929.* Montreal: Études Vivantes, 1982.

Vallières, Gaétan, and Villemure, Marcien. *Atlas de l'Ontario français.* Montreal: Études Vivantes, 1981.

Walker, Franklin A. *Catholic Education and Politics in Ontario.* Toronto: Thomas Nelson and Sons, 1964.

Wallace, Donald C. "Intergovernmental Relations and Language Policy in Ontario." Master's thesis, York University, 1979.

Index

Moulin à Fleur, 5–7, 11, 110, 112. *See also* Sudbury

Newspapers: *Le Droit*, 8, 88; *Le Voyageur*, 65, 67–68
Nouvel-Ontario, xi–xii, 3–4, 10, 38, 40, 51, 95, 125
Nuit sur l'étang, La, 3–5, 7

Official Languages Act, 10
Ottawa, 8
Ouellet, Albert, 89–90, 109–10, 112–14, 119, 122

Paiement, André, 8, 16, 18, 21, 26, 28–33, 104, 131–32. *See also* Theatre
Paquette, Robert, 4, 27–28, 31, 33–34, 95
Parent, Madeleine, 104, 109, 117–19, 120. *See also* Unions
Paris, Robert, 70
Pharand, Arthur, 5. See also *Caisses populaires*
Pharand, Richard, 44, 80
Pilon, Jean-Guy, 30–31
Poetry, 16–17, 141
Prudhomme, Emile, 102, 121–22. *See also* Unions
Publishing, Franco-Ontario: Prise de Parole, 11, 27, 34–35

Quebec: attitudes to Franco-Ontarians, ix, 88–90, 136, 166–67; economic links with Franco-Ontario, 39–40, 47, 165–67; Franco-Ontarian feelings about, 8, 23, 27, 81, 85; nationalism, 39
Quiet Revolution: Franco-Ontario, 3, 16–17, 35; Quebec, 30, 126

Régimbal, Albert, 112, 114. *See also* Centre des jeunes

Royal Trustco, 147–51, 154–55

St-Jean, Lauré, 116–22 *passim. See also* Unions
Savard, Pierre, 81, 88–89
Sturgeon Falls, 4
Sudbury, ix, xi, 3, 5, 8, 9, 10, 74, 78, 84, 97–98, 160. See also Moulin à Fleur
Survivance, la, 53, 57–58, 65–69, 89, 95

Tester, Jim, 99
Theatre, Franco-Ontario, 4–5, 16, 19–32 *passim*, 35, 141; schools, 19–23
Théâtre du Nouvel-Ontario, 24, 28–32, 138
Timmins, xii, 9, 37, 38, 138–39
Toronto, 8
Tremblay, Gaston, 27, 95. See also Publishing

Unions: Confederation of National Trade Unions (Quebec), 102, 120, 135; Employees Association, Dubreuilville, 135–36; Mine-Mill, 9, 98–123; United Steelworkers of America, 99, 102, 105, 106, 109, 111–22
University education: Hearst College, 141; Laurentian University, 3, 40, 65, 67, 80; University of Ottawa, 8, 10, 22

Val Caron, 7

White, Kenneth, 147–51 *passim. See also* Royal Trustco

Youth, Franco-Ontario, 3–5, 19–24, 26–28, 35, 54–55, 83–87, 89, 104

Zorzetto, Paul, 143–44